Ecstatic Ritual
Practical Sex Magick

Twentieth Anniversary Edition

Brandy Williams

Treadwell's

Ecstatic Ritual:
Practical Sex Magick

Brandy Williams

Megalithica Books

Stafford, England

Ecstatic Ritual: Practical Sex Magick
Brandy Williams
© 2008 Second edition

Cover Art: Kris Leet
Cover Design: Andy Bigwood
Editor: Taylor Ellwood
Layout: Taylor Ellwood

Set in Book Antiqua and Poor Richard

Megalithica Books Edition 2008

A Megalithica Books Publication
http://www.immanion-press.com
info@immanion-press.com

8 Rowley Grove
Stafford ST17 9BJ
UK

ISBN 978-1-905713-25-7

Dedication:

To Alex Williams: reaffirmed and renewed in love.

Acknowledgements:

To Ted Gill, who proofreads everything I write, and whose unflagging support makes what I do possible.

To Kallista, who encourages me to be authentic, however frightening that might be.

To my brothers and sisters in the O.T.O., whose initiations and rituals have shaped my magical life.

Other Books by Brandy Williams:

*Practical Magic for Beginners,
Techniques and Rituals to
Focus Magical Energy*, Llewellyn, 2005

Table of Contents

Introduction to the Revised Edition

Since I wrote this book the field of sacred sexuality has virtually exploded. Twenty years ago not much had been published--it was possible to read through the available literature fairly quickly. Now it would be a full-time enterprise to keep up with every book written about sexuality in a magical or spiritual context.

Whole communities have developed which have brought the topic of sexuality out into the mainstream. The sex positive community works to educate people about sexuality and redefine what it is to be "normal". The polyamory community provides a context which permits the expansion of our understanding of relationships and family.

Of course the advent of the internet has played a significant role in these developments. It is much easier today to locate books, track down information, and connect with others who share the same interests. Tantric texts that I searched for in used bookstores for decades are available now online.

In some ways a great deal has changed, but some areas remain untouched. Although there is an openness to exploration in the new communities and a renewed humanist emphasis on the value of every individual, there are those in the sex magick traditions, East and West, who continue to treat sex magick as a form of personal power for the male sex magician, with his female partner serving as a magical tool, a source of inspiration and energy to be sure, but not an equal partner in the enterprise. Traditional sex magick texts ignore or condemn same-sex partnerships and code the color white for spiritual, black for negative. Few writers examine their positions of privilege, of gender, race, age, or orientation, and few make attempts at inclusiveness.

In the last decade a few pioneering writers have looked beyond traditional heterosexuality to expand sex magick into less vanilla areas. Donald Michael Kraig pushed into this new territory with his chapter "Thresholds of Sex Magick" in *Modern Sex Magick*, while Taylor Ellwood and Lupa devoted an entire groundbreaking book to *Kink Magic*.

Twenty years ago only a few women wrote about sex magick, notably Melitta Denning. Fortunately since then more female voices have emerged. Kraig, again, published essays written by women in

Modern Sex Magick. Dolores Ashcroft-Nowicki wrote *The Tree of Ecstasy,* and Lupa co-wrote *Kink Magic.* Although women contributed to the field, even today women's voices are still few and far between. That is one reason I am very happy that Megalithica has chosen to reprint this work.

Although I was tempted to make radical alterations, I have made only conservative changes in this revision. In the first edition of this book I used the term "hetaera" to designate the practitioner of this system. This had advantages and disadvantages. Since it is not a word that had been previously applied to sex magick, it did not catch on, even among users of the system. On the other hand, it did not carry the associations with the idea of the sex magician as one who uses sex as just another magical tool. I was able to define the word to include emotion, relationship, and spiritual engagement, as well as the movement of energy to achieve a result. Although I was tempted to change the term, I have not found another that describes the practitioner of the kind of sex magick developed here.

I have significantly updated the chapter on the magical use of body fluids. Few of the gay men I practiced magick with twenty years ago remain alive today, and a dear friend lost his sister at a traumatically early age. In fact we lost a whole generation of creative and talented magicians to AIDS. Diseases passed through intimate contact cast a cloud on our lives. It is irresponsible for a sex magick writer to write on this subject without firmly addressing the accompanying social and health issues.

One topic that always comes up in discussions and lectures is ethics for sex magicians. Over the years I have developed my own understanding and have engaged in many conversations with other magicians, both beginners and experienced. I explore this topic in the new Appendix Three, Sex Magick Ethics.

The system of sex magick developed here draws on both Western and Eastern sources. Students of Ceremonial Magick will recognize a modified form of the Middle Pillar exercise, the use of the magical personality, and the keeping of a journal. Tantric devotees will recognize the chakras and energy channels in use in various Hindu and Buddhist systems. Some of the material comes from my experience with my partners, a circle of people who worked with some of these ideas, and feedback from students from around the country. I have benefited greatly from information sharing and experience in the growing sex positive community.

All these sources have merged to create an ecstatic ritual, a system in which sexuality is the central form of magical, emotional, and spiritual development. Practitioners truly become companions, growing not just through physical pleasure or magical competence, but through a total engagement of head, heart, body, and spirit, with our partners, with the world, and with our innermost sacred selves.

Brandy Williams
April 2008

Introduction to the First Edition

What is a hetaera?

The term derives from a Greek word meaning companion.

I use the word to mean those of us who own and control our sexuality, fully understanding and embracing its power and potential. Hetaeras make love whenever, wherever, and with whomever we choose, for reasons we consciously acknowledge, with results we skillfully control.

The sexual choices we make span the gamut of human behavior: celibacy, dedication to a single partner of the same or opposite sex, relationships with multiple partners, or making love only with ourselves. We know what we're doing and why we're doing it: taking responsibility for the effects of our choices on our own lives and all those who are affected by them.

Anyone can become a hetaera. Age, weight, sex, race, and physical appearance matter not at all. What does matter is knowledge, skill acquired through practice, and attitude. We practice the magick of sexuality--living in a healthy body with a clear heart open to the touch of the divine.

What you're reading now is a hetaera's training manual, containing exercises which integrate caring for the body, attention to emotion, disciplined imagination and spiritual awareness to form a new approach to sexuality. The exercises and rituals are constructed for use by one person or by any couple.

My partner Alex and I were originally driven to explore sex magick to contain and explain our own sexual experiences. We've spent many years studying the material available on Western sex magick systems, and studying English translations and interpretations of Hindu and Tibetan Tantric texts and practices. Our explorations of ancient Near Eastern and Greek rites fit nicely into what we were discovering about the parameters of this kind of magick. To these we've assimilated our study of Witchcraft traditions and Ceremonial Magick practices. After some years we began to lecture on our discoveries, and to counsel students who approached us to explain what we were doing and how that related to their own experiences.

In the course of teaching we've had the pleasure of trading notes with male and female couples and bisexual people. Through these experiences and conversations we've articulated a value system which underlies every exercise and ritual in this manual.

First: energy is energy. We do not recognize a differentiation between male and female energy, between what heterosexual and same-sex couples experience in magical workings. Everyone has access to the energy that is the source of all life, and the shape of our bodies does not bar us from achieving any sexual skill. Any man or any woman, alone or with any partner, can work through this magical system.

The key to understanding that value is the phrase "magical workings". Of course men and women have different physical experiences. Untrained men tend to achieve climax more quickly than women; training can even out that tendency, allowing both men and women greater control over when climax occurs. Women menstruate, and men do not, physically; but men respond to the moon's phases in more subtle physical ways, and men living with women are entrained to their rhythms.

The biggest difference between men and women physically is that women conceive and bear children. For this we believe women should be honored and understood to be especially sacred. However, responsibility for contraception, and for the control of magical energy which generates a child, is shared by both partners.

Men and women receive different social training, and so our emotional rhythms differ. It is our value that the basic structure of the human psyche remains the same for both men and women, and that our work is to learn from one another to achieve a balance of skills and behaviors our culture labels "masculine" and "feminine".

Second: The most important source of information is personal experience. Trust yourself, even when what you feel and see differs from what you read or have been taught about your sexuality.

Third: the key to successful sex magick is trust and equality. When working with a partner, both of you must benefit from the practice, developing physically, emotionally, intellectually and spiritually.

Finally: you're in charge of your own training, and you decide what you will and will not do, and how quickly. Take this study course at your own pace. It's best to start with the first exercises and work through them in sequence. You may move through some of these assignments quickly until you find a working that requires more time and attention. Or you may proceed slowly, savoring the effects of a blossoming awareness of your body and your body's

Brandy Williams

connections with the earth, with other people, and with the worlds beyond our physical world.

This manual divides into two sections. The White Hetaera focuses on the pivotal skills sex magick requires. The color white symbolizes new beginnings, innocence, and renewal; working through the exercises in this section, you'll find new ways of approaching sexuality and its place in your life.

The color red signifies passion and power. The Red Hetaera section explores specific magical approaches to sexuality--building a magical personality; understanding and controlling the body's energy flows; relating to the divine within ourselves, our partners and the world. The exercises we practice allow us to move into a ritual space, treating sexual experience with the care and respect it deserves.

Paying conscious attention to the arts of love increases our capacity for pleasure. A hetaera moves constantly in the intoxicating atmosphere usually associated with a new love: the knowledge of being attractive, the joy of being courted and gradually revealing ourselves, the shine on the face everyone can see. Aren't I lovely? Aren't I handsome? I am cherished; I am caressed and caress; I am flowers and gold jewelry and fine wine; I possess the finest gift the world can offer, the priceless gift of ecstasy. The difference is that the hetaera's source of joy is the sensuous living world, and the hetaera's lover is life itself.

The White Hetaera

Chapter One: Sacred Sexuality

When I am alone, walking the street, I come aware of the bodies. All the bodies: my friends and lovers wear, and strangers, passing in the street, swarming, surrounding me, supple and strong and swaying with unconscious grace: Serpent, I see your movements in theirs. The eyes. They catch me in passing, fix on me their sorrow and singing joy, clear and conscious and sunk in dream: Serpent, you stare out at me from every face. And I respond. Your devotee, how can I not? turn and touch, now with the hand, again with a word...and when the your call is strongest, there with the whole of my body, my most secret thoughts I worship you. Where I find you: and I find you everywhere.

What is the Snake? The passion within each human body; the experience of that passion, deriving from training and skill; and the symbol for the source of that passion, the Spirit which breathes life into the universe.

A hetaera is a companion of the Snake, a lover who approaches making love with conscious awareness of the magick of the body. Those of us who are hetaeras are reclaiming our sexuality, the life of the body and our joy in it, our presence on the planet and our pleasure.

Sex is the most engrossing human act. Intimate touch involves all the senses. At the moment of pleasure, of shivering contact with a partner or a stolen moment of self-love, all our normal duties, tasks, fears, failures, all the things we *do* drop away. This is life at its simplest, a time simply to *be*--to watch, listen, smell, taste, touch and feel, to focus on being a physical creature and experience the body's capacity for pleasure.

When our bodies are healthy and our hearts clear, when we can give and accept pleasure freely and with sincerity, when we bring to intimate touch an awareness of the divine, sex becomes sacred. We blossom into a fully human consciousness, caught up in a passionate embrace of life.

The culture which raised us did not prepare us for this kind of sexual experience. Our physical training, our habits of thought about sexuality, our religious systems specifically block and diminish our access to the transformative power available to us through physical pleasure. Relearning what many cultures before us have known, that our sexuality connects us to divinity, means articulating a mythology and a magical framework which expresses the experience of a modern hetaera. We are redefining the words, creating new histories, revisioning the gods. We are stepping beyond the limitations which have imprisoned us to reach for an expanded sense of self.

The hetaera commits to living and upholding the values which sustain sacred sexuality. Foremost is the covenant we pledge with our partners and with ourselves:

--My body is sacred. I accept every part of my body. I care for my body.

--I trust myself to enter the process of initiation, of death and rebirth, of renewal, of self---exploration, and to continue to walk the path of my life with integrity.

Next we make a covenant with our partners:

--I dedicate myself to accepting and expressing love, the power of healing, acceptance, the dissolution of boundaries, and the integration of disparate parts.

Love, here, is the journey, and our goal is to become more perfect lovers.

Cherishing our sexuality and consciously augmenting our sexual skill sustains a broader, more confident self-image. Keeping the central self inviolate, sacred, nurturing it, framing it, containing it, feeding it, we learn that from that center life becomes a circle. We walk in a mandala world, seeing life through a lover's eyes. We become warriors of the body, warriors of the night, warriors of the snake--supple, flexible, centered, alive in the moment.

Reclaiming our sexuality as sacred means more than changing our thinking. Bits and pieces of ancient wisdom remain to us, scattered in texts throughout the world. To them we turn for the guides, values, precepts which soften the difficulty of the early lessons. From these we derive our magical system, the study, exercise, and discipline that will reshape our lives--maintaining a healthy body, developing an acceptance of pleasure, and learning specific skills that channel energy. Only then are we prepared to receive the illuminating, disintegrating, resolving force of divinity.

Our first lesson is that sexuality is not simply a physical phenomenon. Our bodies consist of more than blood and skin and bone; energy forms a body within the body. As our physical selves have veins, lungs and organs, so our subtle bodies contain pathways that direct the flow of energy and centers that absorb, collect and direct it.

Sexuality alters the flow of that energy in profound ways. Consciously understanding that process, accepting it, and controlling it turns sex into magick.

When we learn to live within the subtle body, we gain greater control over the physical one. That requires developing the ability to visualize and to sense the movement of energy. We practice controlling our breath, channeling energy within the subtle body, and releasing that energy to achieve an intended result.

So many other disciplines feed into this one. In a sense it's impossible to create a complete description of magical sexuality--our physical pleasure can't be separated off from the rest of a magical life. Dreamwork, guided visualization, creative visualization intended to produce material manifestation, and any martial arts and exercise augments the work we do with magical sexuality.

However, none of these things are essential to beginning to work. You don't have to be an ascended master or study in Tibet to unlock the body's potential--everyone has access to the magick of sexuality. All it takes is beginning the first exercise, and working through each in turn. Remember, too, that while it's important to set goals and achieve them, life is a process, learning any system takes time--and the joy of this lies especially in the journey itself.

Chapter Two: Caring for the Body

Sexuality can't be separated from our enjoyment of physical wellbeing in general. The first magical act that dedicates us to sacred sexuality is commitment to paying attention to the body.

The hetaera's care for the body differs sharply from the health enthusiast approach--lift those thighs, pump that iron, no body that doesn't wear a leotard gracefully is worth looking at, drink only wheat grass juice, and never use any stimulant whatsoever!

Lots of experts seem to have an opinion about what we should do with our bodies and when. They seem to be based on the assumption that all bodies work the same, that we need someone to tell us how to operate it, and that the body is nothing more than a kind of soft machine.

It's time to reclaim our bodies for our own use. This delicate mechanism offers us sensitive feedback on the effects of our diet, our exercise programs, our stress levels and ways of thought that is far more useful than any pronouncement of a health expert. As practitioners of a magical system we also understand the body as a temple of divine force, a unique expression of the most sacred Spirit. We can tune ourselves to listen to the messages of the body when we take the time to do it.

Hetaera Time

As the pace of life accelerates--with career movement, the addition of children to the family--evenings can be as frantic as daily schedules, and weekend events fill the calendar. New demands on our physical strength siphon off leisure time, sleep time, unscheduled time.

For others, those accustomed to a slower pace of life or who live lifestyles outside the mainstream of the dominant culture, keeping a schedule may be a difficulty. When we lose our dependence on the clock we can lose discipline with it.

It's essential for those with busy schedules to mark off time for relaxation; just mark it in red on the calendar if that's what works. One night per week and one weekend per month must remain clear of any other activities. It's not "doing nothing"; you're recharging the physical batteries that allow us to do everything else, and do it well.

Order food brought in or try a finger-food meal. Send the kids out to a movie or hire a babysitter, or combine forces with someone else who can share child-care time. Reduce the list of "things-to-do" relating to work, caring for a family, caring for a home, to zero.

This can be disconcerting, especially to those who become accustomed to having too many items on the list. We pick up the habit of grabbing any bit of spare time to make one more phone call, do a fast-clean of the living room, whip up a bit of dessert for tomorrow's lunch. All of this keeps our lives in control and running smoothly. It may seem that marking off time to care for ourselves will cause the whole house of cards to fall down.

It won't, of course. The list will still be there tomorrow, and the motivation to plow through it won't vanish in an evening. You're making a commitment to yourself, to love yourself first, in order to bring greater love and caring to everything else you do in your life.

On the other hand, an evening a week of free time may seem like a paradise--if it's possible to get. There's always something else to do, something that seems terribly important. That's where keeping your appointment with yourself becomes an act of discipline. You're prioritizing your hetaera training. Get firm about it!

You may need to spend your hetaera time sleeping at first. Those of us on every-minute-taken schedules tend to reduce our sleep-time to less than the minimum. The first job is to bring the body back up to full operating capacity. Watch television, read a book, rent a movie, do something you'll enjoy you haven't found time to do. Relax the body, relax the mind, stretch out and let yourself remember what it's like to enjoy your physical being.

Those with schedules not pegged to a clock, such as artists and the self-employed, generally learn self-discipline in scheduling. We can also find some things seem less important. There's always time, there's always tomorrow. That's when it's vital to make a date with ourselves and keep to it. Our own comfort and happiness is our first priority, and keeping an appointment with ourselves demonstrates that to every part of us and everyone around us.

Hetaera time is dedicated to physical health. When you've gotten enough sleep, when you're accustomed to marking that one night a week or one block of time in a Sunday afternoon to taking care of yourself, it's time to begin the training program.

That means marking off a private space as well. Whether you live alone or with a crowd, pick one particular place to work within. You'll want a space that allows some room for movement, that's comfortable and pleasant for you to use, and that has a door that you can close to keep the world out.

Exercise: Stretching the Body

An exercise program is essential to maintaining a comfortable body. Even manual laborers benefit from a regular program. Start off with doing something physical, something that's easy to do. Learn a muscle-stretching routine, from a friend, from a television or video aerobics program. Turn up the stereo and dance.

You can try the full body relaxation exercise. Lay on your back on a comfortable surface, with your legs stretched out and your arms at your side. Tense your toes as much as you can, then relax them. It helps to inhale while you're tensing, then exhale while relaxing. Now tense your ankle muscles and relax them. Work your way up the whole of your body: your calf muscles, shins, knees, thighs--there are several muscle types there, can you tell the differences? Tense your buttocks, abdomen, chest, lower back, upper back, upper arms, lower arms, wrists and fingers, shoulders, neck, jaw, ear muscles, eye muscles, and scalp, in whatever order you're comfortable with. Then lay there for a few minutes and breathe, sensing the tension run out from your whole body as you exhale, feeling yourself relax with every new breath.

Exercise: Play Time

Pay attention to your body. Take a long shower, or a bath with oil. Try something you haven't tried before--use a loofa or other rough sponge on your skin (it scrubs off dead skin cells), rub yourself with oil or baby powder. Use a moisturizer on your face. Shave your arms if you haven't done it, or grow hair somewhere you haven't. Trim your nails or paint them. Soak your feet in hot water. Henna your hair, dye it, and braid it. Try makeup and perfume or cologne, or change colors or fragrance.

You may be self-conscious at first, and that's okay. Push your boundaries a bit. For now this is a time you spend alone with yourself. Lock the bathroom and don't let anyone in. Experiment with new ways to see yourself, rather than ways you've been told you ought to look. Nothing's permanent; the dye washes out, the polish comes off, the hair grows back or can be cut off. The purpose of the exercise is to help you feel special, worthy of extra attention, to nourish yourself.

Exercise: Learn Your Body Type

What's your ethnic heritage? What peoples went into the mix of bloodlines you carry? That will determine much of your physical appearance. Find out what kinds of bodies go with the strands of your heritage. Do they have broad shoulders or small ones? A tendency to thicken at the waist, or hourglass figures? Long legs or short ones? What color hair is typical? Collect photos of people with your heritage; you can check out books from the library, or look through National Geographic, or pick up some coffee-table volumes.

Do you have photos of your family--your parents, your uncles and aunts, your grandparents? Some lucky souls may have photos of their great-grandparents. Note their physical appearance. How does your body resemble your relatives? How does it differ?

Make a collage of the images you've collected, or paste a few in a place only you will see. All of us are surrounded by images of other people, and our cultures identify only some physical characteristics as beautiful. Those characteristics may not belong to our body types, may not be normal for us. Surround yourself with images of your own people.

For comparison, look at other people as you move through your day. How many sizes and shapes do bodies actually come in? For those who are comfortable with the notion, a nude dip in a hot tub or pool with friends offers an excellent opportunity to look at actual bodies. They're much more varied than the images media normally present us.

What you're doing here is expanding your vision of the human body in general and your own body in particular. That provides the context for learning to accept the body you wear.

Exercise: Love Your Body as It Is

Tackle this exercise at a moment you feel good about yourself. This one you absolutely must do behind a locked door, telling everyone you live with you're not to be disturbed.

Turn the lights down or use candles. Take your clothes off and look in a mirror--a full length one is ideal if you have one, but any largish mirror will do. Think or say these affirmations:

To your feet: I love you. You provide my support in the world and my contact with the earth.

To your legs and buttocks: I love you. You are my strength in the world, and my movement.

To your genitals: I love you. You provide my pleasure and the power of sexuality.

To your stomach: I love you. You absorb my food and nourish my physical being, and give away what I do not need.

To your chest and lungs: I love you. You take in air and purify my blood.

To your arms and hands: I love you. You perform my work and allow me to act in the world.

To your back: I love you. You keep me upright and support all the movement I make.

To your neck: I love you. You house the voice which allows me to communicate to the world.

To your head: I love you. You take in food and air and all my knowledge of the world.

Differently-abled people may want to rewrite some of these affirmations to accurately reflect the redistribution of functions. Pay particular attention to those parts which operate differently from the ones on this list; the affirmations will be most effective with those.

Exercise: Consciousness of the Body

This is a direction of awareness. Consciousness is a function of mind, of course, but most of us experience the "thinking" part of ourselves in a physical location. Where does the observing you reside? Behind the eyes? In the stomach?

Now practice shifting the perceived location of your "I". Focus on a spot two or three finger-lengths below your navel--this is the center of balance in martial arts. Keep awareness of just that point while you breathe slowly. Maintain the exercise for the duration of ten breaths.

Another kind of body awareness teaches us how we hold ourselves. Lie on your back as you did in the full body relaxation exercise. This time check-in with parts of your body. Ask yourself, where am I tense? Check your feet, your legs, lower back, abdomen, upper back, chest, shoulders, upper arms, lower arms, wrists, neck, ears, eyes, and scalp.

Then do the relaxation exercise, or get up and move through your muscle-stretching routine. Doing this once a week for a month or two will teach you where you normally hold tension. Then you can incorporate a stretch or two into your daily routine. As an example, professional typists tend to carry a lot of tension in the shoulders. Getting up from the keyboard every few hours to roll the shoulders can help to relieve much of that discomfort.

Exercise: Observing Movement

As you sit, walk around the room, lie on the floor in hetaera time, notice how you carry yourself. Is your head erect, or do you normally look down? At what angle do you bend your knees? How do you sit-- where do you put your legs? What surface to you lean against, and how much do you bend your back? How does what you are wearing affect your movement? Check the tightness, cut, and weight of your clothes, and your shoe styles.

This is useful information to have as you make your tension check. You may notice that certain postures generate some chronic muscle pain. This is also an exercise you can do as you move through your daily life.

The next section of the exercise you can do whenever you leave your house. Watch people move as they walk down the street. How do they hold themselves? Are the shoulders pushed up toward the neck? Do they take large steps or small ones? How fast do they move?

Can you spot the people who are comfortable with their bodies, and those who aren't? Athletic sorts, bicycle riders, dancers and runners, are especially fun to watch – their movements seem fluid and connected. It's also enlightening to watch older people move. Some seem to experience pain just in walking, while others walk slowly but with grace.

These observations provide information and models for your own work. Looking at a person who walks with hunched shoulders may help bring to awareness your own hunched shoulders. You can see in some older folk that the posture has solidified, and they can no longer hold themselves erect. You can discover what you'd like to improve about your body stance.

Looking at people who seem graceful and comfortable in their bodies can show you how to make the change. How does your body stance differ from theirs? Can you straighten your shoulders, or lengthen your stride a bit?

We've gone beyond acceptance and care for the body now into actually shaping it. While you're making these observations, it's important to hold onto your love for yourself. It's easy to drop from comparison into self-criticism. When you find yourself thinking, gosh what an ugly neck I have, it's time to go back to the affirmation exercise.

Learning to love and accept our bodies, to pay attention to grooming and appearance, to relax and to become conscious of our movements, are the most important foundation to our work. Next, we work on developing the body, which is the physical basis of sacred sexuality.

Exercise: Loving Movement

Pick up a physical discipline. It doesn't really matter which one you choose; any movement system you've been attracted to will do perfectly well. You might choose to do aerobics, learn a dance form, or study a martial art.

This might mean for a while that you devote your hetaera time to an outside activity, if you choose to take a class in the system you'd like to learn. You might also be able to fit an extra activity into your schedule. Some systems are more demanding than others; dancers and martial artists really need to spend a bit of time every day on their disciplines. If you have a very busy schedule, you might just learn an aerobics routine from a video or television show or tape. There are also hundreds of books on various kinds of systems that can get you started.

The important thing is to pick the program that's right for you, one that fits into the amount of time you have available, is easy to begin with and that excites you to do. While it's best to do at least some physical exercise in hetaera time, it's not the end of the world if you decide to skip a night to read a book. Pick it up again in the next session. There's a balance between discipline and self-criticism that's important to keep--hetaera time is a guilt-free activity!

Exercise: Balancing the Diet

Few subjects generate as much guilt as the foods we eat--which foods, when we eat them, why we eat them! The modern world deluges us

Brandy Williams

with information on food. What's good for us? What's safe? What should we eat in what proportion, how much should we eat and how often?

The most important diet to create is the one which sustains a healthy body. That diet will be different for each human being--no generalization will hold true for everyone. In this field, you are the expert, and the most important source of information for you is how you feel.

The first step in creating your personal diet is to keep a food log. Get a small notebook and jot down what you eat and when for a month. If you've already set up a magical notebook, use that. It might be helpful too to note how you feel about what you eat. "Juice--refreshing break." "Raw carrots--virtuous." "Hot fudge sundae--what a treat, but I hear my mother's voice saying I'm indulging myself."

At the end of the month, you can make some generalizations about your eating patterns. First, when do you eat?

Monday-Friday
Breakfast--7:30 like clockwork.
Lunch--anywhere from 11 to 2.
Snacks at least once in the afternoon, no pattern.
Dinner--between 5 and 8, depending on schedule.
Saturday
Brunch--10 to 2, depending on schedule.
Dinner--generally at 7, unless I snack my way through the rest of the day.
Sunday
Brunch--at noon like clockwork.
Dinner--8 at my mom's every week.

Now, what is it you eat, and how much of it?

Meat--chicken mostly, some hamburgers, a bit of fish.
Vegetables--canned garbanzos, frozen corn, fresh lettuce.
Fruit--a banana once in a while.
Grains--lots of bread in sandwiches, some oatmeal, rice with dinner frequently.
Treats--snacks tend to be potato chips and candy bars.
Drinks--coffee in the morning, lots of juice, tea in the afternoon on weekends. Put sugar in coffee and tea. Milk a few times a month.

Your next step is to vary what you eat. Your dietary patterns formed partly in childhood, partly from the information you've received from food experts, partly from the framework of your budget and your schedule. Those patterns were only partly based on feedback from your body. Now it's time to listen to yourself and to find out what pattern of mealtimes, amounts, and types of food really nourish you.

There are some general rules of thumb: fresh foods contain more vitamins than frozen, and frozen more than canned. We generally take in more salt and sugar than our bodies require, and generally do not drink enough liquids, especially water. If you find you don't eat a lot of protein, try eating more of it, and if you eat a lot, cut back. Vary the type of protein; substitute some cheese for meat, try fish or poultry instead of beef, or beef instead of cheese. Do you normally eat a lot of bread? Try rice, and try both brown and white rice. Salad bars are great places to experiment with new kinds of vegetables. You may find that the cabbage you hated in childhood has become an adult treat!

You might try bottled water rather than what comes out of your tap. It's also good to when you travel; water differs from place to place, and the body can take some time to adjust to a new kind.

Make only one change at a time, and notice how you feel. Do you have more energy, or less? Visit a produce stand or a supermarket, taking the time to inhale the aromas, feel the foods and examine them. Is there any food in particular you're drawn to? That's your body's signal that you need something in that particular plant.

Some "foods" really act more as stimulants, like alcohol, coffee, sugar, chocolate. Heavy dependence on any one of those will adversely affect your health. You know what your comfort level is, and when you've exceeded it. When you do, it's important to accept the experience and continue to love yourself, and then notice your discomfort level and let that motivate you to change. If it brings you pleasure, do it! If it brings you pain, why bother?

You may discover that your present diet suits your needs perfectly. You may also find that the expert who told you to eat a low-protein, high-carbohydrate diet hadn't lived inside your skin, and you need milk!

When you've settled on a diet that seems to work well, remember to try new foods or a new combination now and again. Body needs shift as we age, with higher or lower levels of stress, when we change geographical area.

What about aphrodisiacal foods? Many cultures have identified different kinds of foods as having a sexually stimulating effect: oysters, apples, the tusks of obscure African animals. In general, the diet that maintains health produces a body that can be aroused, and the food involved in a sexual encounter is probably the least important of the arousal mechanisms. Sure, chocolate releases endorphins; but is it the chocolate that elevates your pulse, or his big brown eyes?

Exercise: Training for Love

All these exercises are crucial to satisfying sexuality. You might have noticed that stretching and relaxing contribute to greater physical comfort when you make love with yourself or a partner.

This exercise focuses specifically on the genitals. The next time you urinate, practice cutting off the flow of liquid and then releasing it again. That will identify a set of muscles that can benefit from regular exercise.

In hetaera time, practice flexing and relaxing those muscles. Do it just ten times at first; try building up to twenty and then thirty "push-ups".

For men, the exercise will identify a whole range of muscles along the penis and at the perineum-the point between the base of the penis and the anus. Women will identify another set of muscles in the first third of the vaginal walls. Practice contracting and relaxing those muscles as well.

Now contract the anal muscles, and do your push-ups with them. At first the other muscles will contract along with them. Keep doing the exercises until you can contract each muscle group separately.

This is an exercise that's also possible to do anytime, anywhere you're comfortable. The toners form part of a regular hetaera time routine. Women will find that the exercises enable a conscious contraction of the vagina around an object--a finger, a vibrator, a penis. Men will find that the erect penis flexes more easily.

Identifying and exercising those muscles help facilitate climax control, which will be discussed more completely later.

Working with Others

Those who live alone or in situations where private space is taken for granted can mark out hetaera time at will. Those who live with a partner, children, or a group of people accustomed to a lot of interaction may need to be firm in staking out private territory.

You have a right to privacy and personal time! You don't need to let anyone know you're working toward a more flexible sexuality. Share only what you're comfortable with sharing; don't let anyone pressure you into talking about what you're doing. Hetaera time builds not just health, but a sense of personal identity.

Your living mates may especially notice changes in appearance, your exercise program, and experiments with diet. You can keep all of them private if you like and if you have the space. This is a good time as well to include them in what you're doing. You may encounter a great deal of resistance from your living mates to your private time and the changes you make. Stay calm and firm; they may adjust to your new life with time.

If two of you are working through the training together, you should work through these exercises by yourself. You will want to schedule some hetaera time sessions together. You can start your work together by sharing an exercise program and diet construction; this builds a bond of common experience and teaches a great deal about one another's bodies.

Chapter Three: Accepting Pleasure with an Open Heart

Life is a dance! It's about moving, liking how you move, loving where you live, in a body on planet earth. The hetaera's next task is to learn to dance joyfully. That means claiming our sexuality as our own, healing painful experiences, clearing out negative images and messages about our sexuality, communicating clearly with our partners and being honest with ourselves.

Joy is liking the face in the mirror, learning to say, *I deserve pleasure*. For this, we claim complete ownership of our bodies and our touch. Many of us have "learned" our bodies are not our own. Men and women, we know we cannot really know what is in or on the food we eat. We cannot control what happens to our bodies in the workplace. Some work in offices, some in the large downtown towers, so closed and controlled an environment the office cold flashes through the building. Some of us make our living from what our bodies produce, on the production lines where we may be exposed to chemicals whose effect we cannot predict, some in the fields where we may be exposed to pesticides whose effects we cannot predict.

Our governments may legislate what substances we may legally ingest. We may have no choice about bearing children. Contraception may be difficult to obtain; it may not be possible to obtain an abortion.

Women more often, men sometimes, learn a harsher lesson: our sexuality is not our own. We can be touched against our will, or harshly, painfully. We can be raped. We can be stared at. Someone may casually put a hand on an elbow to steer us through the door, as if our bodies were common property.

Taking back control over our bodies takes time and courage, changing habits of thought and behavior, learning assertiveness. As hetaeras, it's our most essential act. The woman who owns herself, the man who owns himself, chooses every touch at every moment.

That's a difficult promise to make to ourselves and keep. It requires letting go of all the reasons we touch and make love aside from the pleasure of the act and intimacy. Parents, spouses, friends ask us for physical reassurance, for hugs and kisses, sometimes when we are happy to give them and sometimes when we need physical space. Strangers on the street touch us casually. It makes such a scene to say no, to move back; isn't it easier to just let it pass?

We have plenty of reasons for engaging in sexuality that have nothing to do with pleasure and union: as a payment, as a way to bind affections, as a duty, as a physical release, as a high. It works! Sexuality gets us the things we want: the dinner or the job, the affirmation of love, the relationship sustained, the argument avoided, the release from discomfort, the rush of sensation.

Yet every time we suffer a touch we have not solicited, every time we join bodies for any other reason than joy in the moment itself, we reinforce our perception of ourselves as powerless and owned by another. We lose trust in our ability to protect ourselves, to love ourselves, to make wise decisions about our lives. We diminish our power and our ability to approach sex in a sacred context.

With our friends, family and acquaintances, it isn't always necessary to be aggressive. You can gently step back, turn away the hand, with a smile or a deflecting comment. With those you love you can also explain what you are doing, and that the result will be that every time you give a hug or a kiss or your body in union you will be totally present and loving.

It's important too to reserve the right to be firm, both verbally and physically, with anyone at all, from the stranger leaping at us from the alley to the love of our lives.

Affirmation One: I Own Myself

Take a mirror and place it in your practice space. You can use one that you already own, or purchase one you'll use especially for affirmations.

In hetaera time, look at the mirror and say:

> *I love myself. I trust myself. I own myself. No one ever touches me without my permission, whatever it takes to make that stick.*

Say this to yourself during every session for two weeks. You can repeat the affirmation in that time period whenever you look into a mirror.

Affirmation Two: I Ensure My Own Safety

Making that promise stick will require learning self defense.

That doesn't have to mean dedicating your next six years to learning a martial art. Check the newspapers, or call a women's center or a martial arts center, to find a simple self defense class. Three hours worth of training and a few minute's thought every day can build an effective self defense ability.

You can, however, choose to learn a martial art for the increased ability to protect yourself, for the excellent exercise, for the training in concentration, and for the practice in moving energy.

If you've never had any self defense training, start now. If you're ever attacked, you need only outrun your opponent to the nearest place of safety.

Always walk in flat, comfortable shoes that are easy to run in. If that means carrying a spare pair with you in your daily life, do it, and make sure you wear them. Practice spotting the next place of safety as you walk down the street. Is there a convenience store? A house with the light on? A group of people talking? If you had to flee your house, where would you go?

You may need to disable your attacker before you can escape. Disabling an assailant doesn't take a lot of skill. First, you want to keep your attacker out of arm's reach, which means kicking. You probably learned to kick to the front as a child. Practice kicking from the side, without telegraphing the move with the rest of your body, in a short sharp jab. In hetaera time, kick out at the wall a few times; or practice on a light pole or a tree in a park, in a place where you know you're not being disturbed.

A side kick will connect with an attacker at about knee level, and a very small pressure will disconnect a kneecap, far less than the force of your weight! A person with a disconnected kneecap won't be following you as you run down the street.

Next, try shouting as you kick. Make it a sharp, loud sound, like "Hah!" A cry can confuse and frighten an attacker, and demonstrates that you're willing to defend yourself.

You may feel silly as you do this. This is normal and wears off. Try it in hetaera time for at least two weeks; if you still feel silly, do it for two more weeks. When you feel comfortable with the movement and the sound, add it to your practice occasionally, to assure yourself you have the skill.

These are exercises to get you started on self defense and to add to your repertoire. It's best to take a course, however brief, if nothing else to look at other people's styles and get some practice.

This is a good time, too, to review your house and car security, both your physical protection and your habits. Always lock your car; when you visit a friend's house at night, ask them to watch you get into your car, and watch your friends when you give them a lift until they lock their own front doors. Make sure all your windows and doors lock.

Finally, the basic rule of personal safety is: do whatever you it takes. If you feel uncomfortable in a particular place or with a particular person, get away immediately. That may mean sometimes looking a bit foolish, or inconveniencing yourself or someone you're with. Your safety is always, always, always worth it.

Some of us have already suffered physical assault: we've been robbed, beaten, attacked, and raped. It's unfortunately a common experience, and leaves us with a lot of emotions to deal with. Working on our personal safety helps to build our trust in ourselves again. The affirmations strengthen our ability to repulse the sorts of people who coerce others into sexual behaviors.

Affirmation Three: I Am Whole

For those with really serious traumas, however far in the past, healing can be necessary. Seek out a therapist; it's a mark of self-respect. You deserve the care and attention a healer can bring you! Also, if any of the exercises in this book make you uncomfortable or call up images, stop immediately and reach for healing.

You must be certain that you trust the therapist. Choose a person you're comfortable with, and give yourself permission to drop them if you're unhappy with their work. Some of the newer forms of therapy, such as Gestalt, Ericksonian hypnosis, and Neuro-Linguistic Programming, are specifically designed to deal with trauma quickly and without pain.

Get whatever distance you have to from the trauma. Do the forgetting. It's okay to forget, to let the pain go, to cleanse, to heal. The person you were then is not the person you are now. Forgive the now-you for not having been there to protect your younger self.

In hetaera time, take a long, soothing bath, paying special attention to yourself. Dress in something comfortable, something that

32

helps you to feel safe. Bring out the mirror, look at your reflection and say:

I am a hetaera. My body is strong and sacred. My body is my magical tool. I deserve pleasure, and I give and receive pleasure. I choose the experiences I have. I am whole.

Affirmation Four: My Life Is Worth Writing About

Diaries aid emotional healing. More, they allow us to explore new aspects of ourselves, giving us a place to communicate thoughts and experiences we could share with no living being. You might pick up a book or two on keeping a journal. Or you may just visit a paper vendor and let the blank volumes themselves inspire you.

The size or type of book you choose isn't important; neither is making a daily entry. Pick a type of journal you'll enjoy using, and write in it whenever inspiration strikes. You can pick out a book that you can carry with you, or work in several books of different sizes and colors.

Sit in hetaera time with the paper in your lap for a while until a thought occurs you'd like to record. Let yourself know how you're feeling, what happened last night, some new things you'd like to try.

From now on, at the end of each hetaera time record the day, the time, and what you did. That will begin to build a record of the changes you make in yourself. Charting your progress is one of the most important magical acts.

The diary helps us to explore ourselves, serving as a safe space to encourage positive change and a sense of power over our lives. In the longer term, of course, regaining control of our bodies means changing our cultures. As magicians, we give ourselves that we have power over how we react to the world, and have the power to alter our context as well.

Affirmation Five: I Can Change My World

Investigate political action groups in your area, and find one whose goals meet your own. Volunteer your hetaera time for two weeks, or even just an hour or two. You may be making phone calls, or licking envelopes, or collating a newsletter.

If group work doesn't interest you, check out a political action newsletter from the library, borrow one from a friend, or write for a sample copy. Inform yourself about an issue that interests you.

Almost every copy of such magazines contains a call to write letters or donate money, which provides an avenue for action. Or you can simply put together information about the issue and pass it on to two or three friends, bringing it to their awareness.

At the end of that period, it's important to suspend your political activity; it's addictive, and can eat up large periods of time. Take your practice back for hetaera work; then, if you choose, you can add further volunteer activities to your life. In your practice space, in hetaera time, look at yourself in your mirror and affirm:

I am powerful. I act to make positive change in my world. I act to ensure that everyone owns their own bodies.

Affirmation Six: My Body Is Beautiful

Owning our sexuality as well as our bodies may take some re-thinking. We've picked up attitudes toward sexuality, through family and cultural training, media messages, and a lack of information and support, that seem designed to alienate partners and minimize enjoyment of sexual experience.

In "Real Man School", boys learn competitiveness. The biggest genitals, the fastest climax, and the farthest spurt of semen wins. Boys control what's going on. That means that sex is only for male enjoyment, and it also means that boys never lose control, never show emotion. The winner is the one who can operate the machine most efficiently, car, computer, or human body.

Other messages, in some ways more positive but still competitive and goal oriented, add a layer of conflicting signals to boy training. The man who "get it on" the longest and stays the hardest wins. You have please your gal, you have make her come, you have to make her come more than once. You have to be the best she's ever had.

"Girl School" teaches a whole other set of set of behaviors, some competitive, some placating. Looking good is more important than comfort. The most expensive dress, the most careful make-up job, the neatest grooming wins. Give him what he wants no matter what it is or how you feel about it. Never win a game with a man, never let him know you're in control. Here too there are the conflicting messages: Don't enjoy it, but you have to come 12 times a night. It's not real unless it's intercourse. Don't tell him what you want, ever.

Increasing ability and enjoyment involves taking conscious control of our training, giving ourselves permission to move beyond the limits "real man school" and "girl school" taught us. The hetaera seeks maximum behavioral flexibility. Giving up control to a partner, or completely directing a session. Spending hours simply stroking the skin, or in full and intense intercourse. Remaining sensitive to a partner's moods and needs while clearly communicating our own needs and goals.

Often we refer to body parts and to sexuality with words that emphasize the negative attitudes our culture instills. Hetaeras make a commitment to change our descriptions. We draw our new language from the better English phrases, from the natural world, from our own observations of our bodies, and from cultures which have described bodies and sexuality in more positive terms.

In hetaera time, look at your genitals in the mirror. Describe yourself either mentally or aloud. What colors do you see? What shapes and textures?

Some metaphors that you can use:
For **vulvas:** flower; gate; the curve of a mountain or a rock; a cup, containing and giving off fluids; silk and satin, for the walls of the vagina; the pearl in the oyster, for the clitoris.
For **penises:** staff; stalk; trunk; stone spire; the vine, for the series of veins on the shaft; the eye or the little mouth, for the opening at the tip.
For **body fluids:** honey; ambrosia; sweet nectar.

Again, any self-consciousness you might experience at first will fade as you reinforce the affirmations, building the knowledge that your body is as beautiful as the plants and animals of the natural world, and sacred.

Affirmation Seven: I Know What I Like

Next in hetaera time, take out your journal. Look honestly at the kinds of sexual behaviors you enjoy, both alone and with a partner. Do you enjoy these behaviors a lot or a little? Every time you make love or only once in a while? Here are some examples:

Giving oral sex. Getting oral sex. Anal penetration, penetrating anally. Heterosexual intercourse. Getting manual stimulation, giving manual stimulation.

Lots of stroking or not a lot; talk, no talk; looking, listening, or not; being looked at, being listened to, or not.

Time of day, day of week. Setting: indoors, outdoors. Soft surfaces or hard ones. Level of light and kind of light.

Parts of body, hair, face, arms, breasts, touched, by hands, by lips.

Now repeat the list for what you specifically do not enjoy, often or ever.

Next, examine your behavior patterns. Do you most often initiate an encounter? How? Verbally, or with a touch signal? Do you most often respond to someone else's request? What triggers your self-love session? Do you always, sometimes, never respond when you really don't want to? Do you tell your partners what you like and don't like?

Think about your sexual history. When did you first make love? What are your sexual milestones? What moments in your life reflect changes in your sexuality? What did you like as a child?

Hetaeras work on expanding the capacity for pleasure. When sexuality has meant so many different things, pleasure gets tangled up with many other physical and emotional needs which the act of lovemaking itself might not meet. Bad experiences with partners can also make us a little wary of physical and emotional fireworks. The net result is that we learn to contract around pleasure, to mistrust it, to limit it to a short period of time. We may even make love with ourselves and others in order to achieve the fastest possible climax, missing out on the joy and power of sensual touch.

Affirmation Eight: I Love Myself

Make love with yourself in hetaera time. Set up a comfortable nest in your practice space. You know what kind of surface you like to sit against or lie on, what level and kind of light you enjoy, and what temperature is most comfortable for you. You might equip your space with pillows or tapestries. Candles cast a gentle light and create a warm atmosphere. You can try burning incense, or rubbing oil on your skin.

Supply yourself with a basket of toys. You might start with a square of silk, something furry, a stone, feathers, as many different textures as you can assemble. Stroke your skin with the toys. On hot days take a quick shower and lie down without toweling off; or you can perform the whole exercise in the tub. Stroke yourself softly, or with pressure; you can experiment with pinching and hitting yourself. Touch parts of your body that you pay less attention to-- your feet, behind your ears, the backs of your knees.

Let yourself know that you love yourself, that you can accept pleasure for its own sake. Make a deal with yourself: the next time you feel the urge to make love with yourself, do it. You may retire to the bathroom in your home or workplace; you may be walking in the woods; you may be having a conversation with a friend; wherever the mood strikes you, excuse yourself for a few minutes and bring yourself pleasure.

Working with Others

In claiming our bodies, we need to let our families and partners know what we want in case of emergency. There are times when laws treat us as incapable of making decisions for ourselves--when we're ill, when we're unconscious, when we're giving birth if we're women. At those times parents or spouses may be called upon to make decisions about what will happen to you. Let them know what you want, and keep talking to them until you're certain they'll follow your wishes. We all deserve respect, especially concerning control of our bodies. In working with partners, this means clearly communicating what we need and want, and building trust.

Building the communication that allows trust and the trust that forms the foundation for intimacy is a long process. It doesn't happen instantly, without effort, and with short-term lovers. But it does happen, and with more than one lover or friend, if you have the heart.

First, you have to be willing to be honest with yourself, to admit your anger, fear, jealousy, need. Next, you must make a commitment to one another always to be honest and always to communicate what you need sexually and what you feel about sexuality. Love doesn't mean reading minds. If you haven't expressed verbally, loud and clear, what you want and don't want, your partner is not responsible for giving you what you need.

Exercise: Establishing Trust Space

Use your next shared hetaera time to create together a place for your hearts to meet gently. Inside trust space there is safety and peace; both partners must be committed to maintaining the space.

The rules are: one person talks first while the other listens without comment or interruption. Then it's the other partner's turn. No part of the discussion ever leaves the room.

Stay centered in the here and now. Use the word "I" a lot--"I feel angry, I'm happy, I'm peaceful right now." This is especially important in flagging behaviors you're asking your partner to change. It's out of bounds to say "you made me feel angry." Remember, as magicians we control our responses to our world and our experience. It's clearer, less threatening, and actually closer to the truth to say, "I am uncomfortable with this behavior of yours. I have this emotion about it."

Begin with sharing as much of your list of sexual likes and dislikes as you're comfortable with. Read them out loud to each other.

Now that your partner knows about your never-likes, stop engaging in the behaviors immediately. Now that you know about your partner's never-likes, offer them the courtesy and love to cease to ask for or expect them. This also allows you an opportunity to give your partner more of what he or she likes.

The commitment to trust and intimacy means releasing old history and accepting one another's foibles. Every day is a new one. Yesterday's anger, sorrow, pain washes away. Held grudges poison; the dawn brings a new chance. Remember too, your partner's flaws make them who they are. Hating those characteristics separates you; cherishing and accepting them builds deep bonds of release, trust, and commitment, and breaks the barriers to union.

Exercise: Calling Time Outs

You've already promised yourself as a hetaera that you will choose every touch at every moment. That may mean that you'll begin a lovemaking session, and discover at a certain point that you no longer want to continue that level of touch.

Partners grant to one another the right to call a time out. As your lovemaking becomes more magically skilled, there will be moments you'll generate more energy than you want to handle. You may want to stop to examine a new perception or a surfacing memory. Or you may just discover that you're too tired or feeling too ill after all.

In that case, communicate to your partner immediately what the problem is as clearly as you can. You might find yourself saying, "I'm scared". What's scared? Focus in on your body's messages. Is there tension in your shoulders? A hollow feeling in the stomach? It's a much more fruitful exploration than trying to figure out what your partner is doing to frighten you. Communicate your sensations to your partner. "My shoulders are tense." At that point you might just ask your partner to rub your shoulders. You can also ask to stop the lovemaking for now.

Of course it's best to be certain you'd like to make love before you start a session. Make sure your physical blood sugar is adequate to the occasion. The body burns up quite a lot of calories in lovemaking, and releases chemical--adrenalin, endorphins. Your body chemistry alters. If you haven't eaten, you'll notice! Drink milk, eat cheese, eat a piece of fruit.

If there's something you haven't said to your partner, you'll also notice it here, especially when you engage in sex magick. Check in on your comfort level: is the problem something you can set aside from now, or is it really diminishing your trust in your partner and your joy in the experience? In that case, close it down.

Each partner has the right to call a time out whenever you need to. For partners with clear communication, this will be an occasional occurrence. Partners without clear communication or adequate trust may use this out often. This is a signal to go back and talk to one another in trust space.

Reasons you might call a time out: a physical problem. You've discovered you can't allow intimacy because of a communication you must make with your partner and this is not the appropriate time. Or, you might discover that there is a resistance in yourself, that you are not yourself clear on what you want to do.

You may feel that the reason you are calling the time out isn't as critical as keeping the connection going. It's always your choice. If you feel it is not your choice, that you are being pressured or threatened or coerced, resist! You have the right to choose every touch at every moment. If there is an issue you feel that you can work through later, you can postpone the discussion or your meditation until after the lovemaking is over.

Calling a time out can be an easy thing to do or a painful one. You may feel guilty or ashamed. You are committed to this person and want them to be happy. Remember that you have the right to choose every touch at every moment. More than that, if you force yourself to accept a touch past a resistance in yourself, you may become less willing or able to accept touch from that partner in the future. Instead of breaking intimacy, calling a time out might *save* your intimacy.

When you call a time out this is the appropriate moment for assurances. "I love you. I care about you." Both partners must affirm this. You may offer your partner a reason for the time out, but this is not necessarily the best time to discuss what is happening in detail. Make an appointment to talk it out in trust space. Then keep the appointment! If you both want to do it now, get up and go to your practice space; break the association between the place you make love and the place where you work out a difficulty.

When your partner calls a time out you may feel irritable, disappointed, angry, hurt. What's the problem? *You're* fine. Acknowledge the feelings to yourself. Of course you're disappointed! Also, do you care about your partner? If you were expressing the need to stop, what response would you want? Give that response. Reassurance, acceptance, and forgiveness are the lover's gifts.

Exercise: Your Body is Sacred

In hetaera time, look at your partner's genitals, and describe them. What colors, textures, shapes do you see? Use the metaphors in the section above. Now let your partner look at your genitals and describe them to you.

Practice looking into each other's eyes and trading affirmations:

Your pleasure is my pleasure. Pleasure is in touch. I love to touch you. My body is sacred. Your body is sacred.

Make a commitment to each other to use positive language to describe each other's bodies and your lovemaking.

As hetaeras, we make commitments of love to ourselves in order to create our magick. The covenant we make with ourselves is to love ourselves: to center in the devotion to sacred experience, honoring our bodies as temples of spirit, our emotions as reflections of spirit, our aspiration as the adoration of spirit for spirit.

The covenant we make with our lovers is to center in the devotion of the sacred within them: to worship their bodies as temples of the spirit, to honor their emotions as reflections of spirit, then encourage their aspirations as expressions of spirit.

Chapter Four: Containing Energy

As magicians we learn first to take control of our physical lives. All our work must ground in a practical result. However, the worlds beyond the physical are our rightful domain as well. We learn to move in what are called the astral or star-worlds which lie within and beyond this one.

We move in those worlds in what's called the astral body, inner body, or subtle body. Working with the subtle body doesn't have to involve learning astral projection, or consciously leaving the physical body, although it can. It's much more important, though, to get a thorough grounding in living in the astral body while it's still firmly implanted in the physical one. After all, that's the state in which we live most of our lives.

Just as we can study the placement of organs and the number of bones in a physical body, we can study the general structure of the subtle body, its channels and centers. You might have seen books on theosophy, polarity, or acupressure, or Yoga which give diagrams of the channels and centers. If you've seen more than one book you may have noticed a difference their descriptions.

One way of explaining the difference in systems is, astral bodies differ. It makes sense that since the physical body is unique the subtle body has its own special structure.

Explore various exercises and give them a fair try. You may discover that your understanding of your own centers differs from any of the descriptions you read, or that energy moves in your subtle body in a different way. Trust yourself and your perceptions of yourself, and work with the flows and centers you perceive. The general rule, here as with any magical system, is: if it works for you, use it.

You may also find after practicing subtle body exercises for a while the structure of channels and centers makes more sense to you, and that your perception of them has heightened. You can try returning some exercises that haven't made sense before to see if they'll work for you now. The important thing is to keep practicing, explore new sources of information, maintain an open mind, and place greatest confidence in your own experience.

The Structure of the Subtle Body

The subtle body extends beyond the visible body; that aura is what psychic healers see, describe, and photograph. It doesn't simply extend from the skin; it underlies the whole of our physical frame.

Just as the physical body has a network of blood and lymph vessels of various sizes, the subtle body contains a network of energy pathways. The major energy conductor runs along the spine, from the genital region out the top of the head.

This central column supports concentrations of energy, centers which approximately correspond to organs in the physical body. Each has a particular function in opening us to types of energy and in controlling emotional and spiritual experiences. The crown center hovers above the top of the head; the forehead center, also called the third eye, sits at the center of the brow; the throat center surrounds the soft spot in the neck; the heart center lies directly between the breasts; the balance center is the point three finger lengths or so below the navel; the genital center sits directly at the genitals; the base center is between the feet.

Minor centers cluster along these pathways and the sense organs, at the eyes, ears, nose, mouth, palms of the hands, shoulders, solar plexus, at the diaphragm, hips, and soles of the feet.

Energy Flows in the Subtle Body

The subtle body takes in energy which flows along the channels and concentrates in the centers. Energy flows from the earth through the soles of the feet, and from the sun and moon. Unless consciously directed these energies distribute first diffusely throughout the auric "egg".

We take in energy when we breathe as well. Yoga and martial arts disciplines have names for this energy: prana, ki of the universe, and others. This energy flows into minor channels and spreads again through the whole of the subtle body.

In addition to taking in energy, the auric skin throws off excess energy. We exhale excess and negative energies. Feet serve as natural grounding devices; the hands can also ground when we touch them to the earth.

We encourage health in our physical bodies by exercise and proper diet; in the same way, we encourage health in our subtle bodies by working and feeding them. Exercise, in this case, means controlling and augmenting the flow of energy in the channels and centers by visualizing and sensing it.

Exercise: Accepting Spirit

Standing in the center of your practice space and facing east, take several deep breaths. Visualize the crown center as a globe about five inches in diameter, suspended a few inches above the head. On an in-breath, imagine white light moving down from the globe through the central column to a globe, again about five inches around, directly between the feet. Sense the warmth the light brings to the central column.

Establish a regular breathing pattern. Try inhaling and exhaling for four or six heartbeats, holding breath and resting for two. When you've completed a few cycles of this pattern, repeat the energy accepting exercise.

Repeat the exercise in practice time for at least two weeks; you might also add it to your regular practice, beginning every session with it. The most primal force of Spirit enters the subtle body through white light and breath. It's one of the most basic in the hetaera's repertoire; it strengthens, balances, and grounds the subtle body.

Exercise: Drawing Earth Energy

Stand beneath a tree. Breathing slowly and evenly, visualize and feel roots growing out from your feet. How far down can you sense them extending to the earth? When you've reached your comfort level, feel and visualize the roots drawing back up to return to your feet. Allow them to grow up along your legs to the balance point just below your navel. Then shake yourself out a little.

This exercise draws the energy of the earth into our bodies. Try repeating it again in your regular practice space. Do you see the light as a different color? Does it have a different feeling to you than the white light drawn in through the crown?

These movements begin a process of cleansing, connection, and balance in the subtle body. Drawing the flame of spirit through the crown to the feet strengthens the central column, and helps to balance all the centers along the channel. Drawing earth energy up into the body strengthens our contact with the energy of our planet, providing a solid foundation for further work.

Exercise: Drawing Solar and Lunar Energy

Aside from the earth, the moon and sun constitute the largest masses in our environment, the most powerful sources of energy. You'll note similarities and differences in the effects of those energies on your subtle body and your heart.

Women in particular, but all of us, are already affected by the moon, whose powerful pull rules the menses and the tides. Of course life on the planet would be impossible without the sun's light, which also provides our physical bodies with vitamins, a tangible nourishment.

The next time you have an opportunity to practice in a natural setting during the day, stand in the sun's rays. Visualize and feel your energy field, your aura, extending from the body. How far does it extend?

Now imagine the yellow or golden light falling gently on the outside of your energy shell and being absorbed into your entire body.

During the next full moon, stand outside and visualize and feel the silver light entering the subtle body.

Working with the Centers

Magical systems assign different colors and geometric figures to the centers. One of the systems associates some of the centers with the elements of the quartered circle.

The base center between the feet represents our contact with the earth. Some systems consider the anus to be the location of this center; when you sit on your heels with the toes of your feet overlapping, the two are brought together. This can make visualization easier if you use more than one system. The element earth can be symbolized by a square, yellow, green or brown in color.

You can visualize the genital center as a serpent with its tail in its mouth, or as a flame. Whichever fits your preference, the eternity symbol works well as a representation of the sexual force. It can be red or lavender in color.

The balance center corresponds with the element air, which can be visualized as a silver upturned crescent.

Fire, the next element, can be represented as an upright red triangle placed in the heart center.

The throat center corresponds with the element water, visualized as a blue circle.

A purplish or indigo oval visualized in the forehead center represents our first psychic opening to the intuition of Spirit. The crown center's white globe symbolizes our contact with Spirit.

Exercise: The Center Meditation

In hetaera time, stand in the center of your practice space. Imagine each of the centers as a colored globe about five inches across: the white crown, the indigo forehead, the blue throat, the red heart, the silver balance, the red or lavender genitals, and the yellow, green or brown base center.

When you're comfortable with this, place the geometric image in each of the centers. There are two ways you can do this: imagine each globe as white, with the shape in its appropriate color; or imagine the globe in color, with the geometric shape in white. Practice just these visualizations for several weeks.

Next, combine these visualizations with the Accepting Spirit exercise. Breathing slowly, imagine and sense white light flowing from the crown through each of the centers in turn. After another two or three weeks with this exercise, establish a regular breathing pattern again and draw the white light through the centers.

This exercise contains more complicated visualizations than previous ones. Some will find it simple to visualize, while others will insist they cannot make internal pictures, and rely entirely on feeling or sensing energy.

Every sighted person visualizes; it's part of our thinking process. Some of us are consciously aware of this, and others are not. Practice will bring the faculty to conscious attention.

Learning to both visualize and internally sense energy is essential to sex magick practice. Expanding conscious awareness of the internal "senses" enormously increases effectiveness both magically and in daily life. We unlock reservoirs of power when we begin to use the faculty least in awareness. For those who visualize easily, bodywork in general will generate new and intense experiences, while for those who are comfortable with their bodies will find in visualization a potent new tool.

Exercise: Visualization Practice

If you'd like to sharpen the skill, try drawing these shapes or cutting out them out from construction paper and pasting them on a white background. In practice time, look at one of the shapes for a few minutes, and then close your eyes and try to see it in front of you. With your eyes closed, roll the eyeball up slightly and imagine the shape projected on a screen slightly above and beyond the eyes.

Work on just one of the shapes for a few practice sessions, and then move on to the next one.

Energy Blockages in the Subtle Body

You might find that your visualization and internal feeling sticks or slows at a particular center. This is a sign that energy is blocking at that point; working through subtle body exercises may bring one or more energy blocks to our conscious awareness.

Channels and centers can become blocked for a variety of physical and emotional reasons. Energy bypasses those areas, putting strain on the channels and centers surrounding the block--rather like a muscle strain when a vertebrae pops out of place. Healers of the body work with the block, loosening the knot so that energy may flow freely through the channels again. Healers of the spirit work with the emotional block, offering new ways of looking at the past and the present to provide more choices in behavior, so that the block will loosen and will not recur.

Sometimes the exercises themselves will loosen the dam and allow energy to flow freely again. This can be an emotional experience, and you may find yourself laughing or crying during early sessions. Sometimes the block persists, and that's a good time to seek the help of a physical or emotional healer.

It's important to note too that you may not notice any blocks. Either you haven't acquired any, or they're too minor for you to notice with newly awakened subtle senses.

Where the blocks occur can point your focus toward particular exercises and changes in behavior. Do you have a block in the base center? How do you feel about your body, your place in the world? You might try working with the Training for Love exercise for a blocked genital center, or changing your sexual patterns--quit engaging in sexuality for a while if you've been doing a lot or make love with yourself or your partner if you haven't. A block at the balance center indicates a need to increase physical exercise, or to work again through Balancing the Elements.

Is there a knot in the heart center? Look again at the accepting pleasure exercises, and try working through them again. Do you love yourself? Is love going out from you to the people around you?

A block in the throat center can indicate you're holding back something you need to say. Do you notice a bit of tension in the forehead center? How do you see yourself? Are there ways in which your perception of the world is preventing you from achieving peace and power?

If you feel pressure or see a block at the top of the head, you might want to pay more attention to creating sacred space and affirming the divine without you and within you.

Sexuality alters subtle body energy flows in a number of ways. We generally give off at least some energy during climax; we can send out quite a bit of energy. As magical workers, our job is to control the amount we take in, where it goes, and how much it gives off.

Exercise: The Personal Circle

We begin to contain energy by strengthening the outer skin of the auric shell.

Start with the Accepting Spirit exercise. Next, sit comfortably in your practice space. If you feel the need for more energy, you can try the Concentration Breathing exercise, drawing more white light into the auric field.

Place your hands in front of the heart center and a few inches away from it. Now circle yourself--raise your hands over your head, draw them down the back, run them along the floor and bring them up to the starting point.

While you're doing this, imagine and sense white light spreading from your fingertips to form a glowing white egg around you. Let yourself know you're surrounded by the protection of the Most Sacred Spirit, however you name that force.

Sit in the circle for a few minutes, relaxing in the serenity of that protection. Now place your hands together above your head. Gradually bring your hands down until they're touching the floor, visualizing and feeling the white egg descending until the floor absorbs it. Remember, it's just the extra protective energy you're grounding; the experience will strengthen the aura.

You can draw the personal circle whenever you do any meditation, or whenever you need to center yourself and touch the peace of the Spirit's protection.

Exercise: Sealing the Centers

In hetaera time, sit in a comfortable position. With the fingers of both hands, touch each of the major centers in turn, from the crown to the base. As you do so, visualize each of the centers just as a colored globe. See the globe closing, like a flower folding its petals together; like a sphincter shutting; use any visualization of a round object closing a door that works for you.

This acts to seal, or contain, the energy of each center within the subtle body system. While the center is sealed, it can only receive or give off energy to other parts of the subtle body.

Now draw the circle around yourself. Sit quietly for a few minutes. Do you experience your subtle body differently than before?

Bring the circle back down around you, this time also visualizing and feeling the centers opening again.

Practice this for a few weeks. Next, seal the minor centers along with the major ones--crown, eyes, ears, nose, mouth, throat, heart, nipples, solar plexus, balance, hips, genitals, anus, soles of feet, and the palms of the hand in turn. The next time you make love with yourself, draw the circle and seal the centers first; when you've finished, ground the circle and open the centers again.

Many emotional swings during the course of lovemaking can be traced to alterations in the energy flow. Sealing the centers and drawing the circle around yourself and your partner can have a profound and immediate effect on your sexual experience. You're no longer losing energy; now you're containing it within the subtle body system. It will immediately work to strengthen the whole subtle body in general.

Sealing the centers and circling the body provides basic magical protection for the hetaera. You may find that you practice the technique sporadically at first; its best, though, to make it an invariable habit, and later workings will require this.

Working with Others

The hetaera's first ethical rule is: never work with a partner's energy without your partner's conscious, verbal, explicit understanding and permission.

If a sexual partner does not practice the system with you, any magical work you do must be limited to yourself. You can seal your own centers, and form a circle around your own body and your partner's body. Putting your arms or legs around your partner and visualizing and sensing the circle will act to draw the egg around you both.

This acts simply to protect you and the energy you're beginning to generate and contain, and acts to protect your partner. This is the full extent of the work you can do with someone who is not practicing sex magick with you.

Warning: sex magick is a satisfying, powerful, and transforming system. If you continue to develop your skill, you will almost definitely find making love with a non-practicing partner to be increasingly unsatisfying. As your skills grow, the temptation to move your partner's energy grows with them.

Partners who work the system together can practice visualization with each other.

Exercise: Shared Centers

In your next practice time together, sit comfortably and face one another. This works best if you're both nude. Visualize the centers on each other's bodies.

Lie next to one another and press your bodies together, face to face. This brings the subtle bodies in contact, interpenetrating. The centers in each body touch and gradually merge with one another. Practice sensing the shared centers.

The next time you make love, practice sealing and circling one another. Touch or kiss your partner's centers with the appropriate visualization and sensation. Then, facing your partner, bring your hands up over their head, down their back, along the floor or bed, up along your back, over your own head, and back to the starting point. Now ask your partner to repeat the movement.

It's again best to practice this each time you make love; eventually it becomes a requirement for further practice. You don't have to stop the show to practice the technique. You can gradually

Brandy Williams

seal each of the centers, and make the circle, in the course of exploring one another's bodies in intimate touch.

Sealing the centers and circling the bodies protects each of you from energy loss. When you move into touching, your subtle body fields interpenetrate. They're still not losing energy, but can now exchange energy. When you press your bodies together, the centers also open to one another; still sealed from energy loss, they now exchange energy with each other. Consciously visualizing and sensing this process builds a powerful awareness of union between lovers.

Chapter Five: Fire Rises in the Body's Temple

Sexual magick focuses on visualizing and sensing energy rising in the central column of the subtle body during lovemaking, and especially during climax.

We use the metaphors serpent and fire to describe that energy, which is generated by the body and by sexuality itself. It's one of the great mysteries of life, one of our primary sources of joy, purpose, nourishment, spiritual awakening.

Exercise: The Serpent Rises

When you've practiced energy containment for several months, get comfortable in your practice space. Seal the centers and circle your body, and make love with yourself. As you do, imagine and sense a white or golden energy rising up the central column of the subtle body from the genital center to the crown. When you have climaxed, see and feel the energy now stored in the crown center as your body relaxes.

Concentrating on the internal image and feeling takes some time and some practice. That's why it's most convenient to start with just making love with yourself, even if you practice with a partner. You can control the rate of your excitement, and the type of stimulation you give yourself. With a partner, it's easier to lose focus and to be swept away with the physical sights, sounds and sensations. If this happens, even with yourself, enjoy the experience! Try it again the next time you make love with yourself.

The serpent's rise tends to be an intense experience. The energy may pool at a blocked center, giving the subtle body a full or bloated feeling. You might also find that your body begins to tremble or jerk slightly. These are normal experiences; they are signs, though, that you should immediately stop your practice and return to the Accepting Spirit and center meditations. Those will clear the blocks, balance the centers, and strengthen the subtle body to handle the new level of energy.

Breathing the Fire

Breathing meditation controls the speed and force of the serpent's rise. Breathing forms our most intimate, heartbeat by heartbeat connection with our physical environment. Control of breathing also forms the foundation of many a magical skill.

Many people use only a small percentage of their lung capacity. Breathing meditations teach us to push out the diaphragm, taking in more oxygen and flushing out the body's impurities.

Consciousness alters with the type of meditation. Long slow breaths oxygenate the blood, expanding our ability to see, hear, smell and feel the world around us. Short fast breaths increase the carbon dioxide level in the blood, contracting sight, hearing smell and feeling to that our immediate surroundings. Meditations on the breathing process teach the mind to focus on a single thing, increasing our ability to concentrate.

Exercise: Deep Breathing

First, find a comfortable sitting position. You can cross your legs or sit on your heels. Next, find your pulse. Check the blood vessels in your wrist, your inner elbow, or your neck.

Now inhale for ten pulse beats; hold your breath for two beats; exhale for ten beats; and rest for two beats. Inhale through your nose, and exhale either through your nose or your mouth.

When you hold your breath, relax your throat. There's a natural tendency to close the throat, holding the breath in. If you open the throat, you'll notice you'll push down on the diaphragm more firmly in order the hold the air in the lungs. Now when you exhale, push the diaphragm a bit and see if you can't push out an extra bit of air. Also keep the throat open (avoid the glottal stop) while resting before the inhalation.

You'll probably notice as you continue the exercise that your heartbeat will slow. This is normal; just go ahead with the exercise. You'll probably also find that you become aware of your heartbeat, feeling the pulse in your chest, and won't have to hold your hand to your wrist or neck to continue to sense it.

You're working here to exercise the diaphragm and related muscles in the abdomen in order to breathe more deeply and with greater ease, and to completely flush and refresh the air in the lungs.

Repeat the exercise ten times, and then stop. Do this in hetaera time for two weeks. If you can, do this every day for that time. You can do some of the other breathing exercises too, or take them one at a time.

Exercise: Controlled Breathing

Again sitting in a comfortable position, inhale for ten pulse beats. Now exhale in a single pulse beat, forcefully expelling the air from the lungs. Inhale again, this time for nine pulse beats, and exhale to the count of two. Inhale for eight beats, and let your breath out in three pulse beats.

Inhalation	Exhalation
10	1
9	2
8	3
7	4
6	5
5	6
4	7
3	8
2	9
1	10

Inhaling for a single beat is called a drop breath; push out on the diaphragm forcefully to create the vacuum in the lungs. Try this exercise in hetaera time for two weeks.

Exercise: Concentration Breathing

When you worked on consciousness of the body you focused awareness on the balance point in the abdomen, two or three finger widths below the navel.

Now combine this with deep breathing. Inhale for ten heartbeats, hold the breath for two heartbeats, exhale to the count of ten and rest for two, keeping your mind on the balance point. You can visualize a small dot there, and try to feel the muscle tension and the air temperature against the skin at that point.

If your mind wanders from the balance point, throwing up images or sensations or concentrating on sounds in the environment, return as soon as you remember to concentrating on the balance point. You might try cutting down on distractions in your environment. Work in comfortable clothes in a warm room; close your eyes; and use earplugs to block out sounds.

Repeat this ten times, and then get up and stretch. Do it in hetaera time, or every day if possible, for two weeks.

Next, add a cleansing visualization to this. As you exhale, imagine all the impurities in your body streaming out from your lungs. On the rest between breaths, visualize white light clustering at your nostrils. Then as you inhale, imagine the white light flowing into your lungs. As you hold your breath, see the light expand to fill your entire body.

Once more, repeat this ten times during your practice sessions for two weeks.

Exercise: Serpent Breathing

In hetaera time, establish a rhythmic breathing pattern to four or six heartbeats. Make love with yourself, imagining and sensing the golden or white light rising in the central column. After climax, again place the energy in the crown center.

Your breathing will probably speed up and grow erratic as you approach climax, and you may find yourself holding your breath. That's normal too; remember, slow breathing oxygenates the blood, while rapid breathing builds up carbon dioxide. Increased oxygen expands our awareness of the information coming in through the physical senses; what we see, hear, and feel around us. Increasing the carbon dioxide concentration in the blood tends to contract awareness to immediate sensations and visions. Each of us has a particular mix of sensations that help trigger the moment of climax; changes in the breathing rate generate that mix.

With practice you'll be able to maintain rhythmic breathing until the moment of climax. This also helps to bring climax more closely under conscious control. Remember to record the results of each exercise in your journal.

Working with Others

Do the breathing exercises alone for the first two weeks. Then you can try doing them in your shared practice time. Try sitting with knees just touching and watching each other breathe (look at the abdomen) and listening for the inhalation and exhalation. You'll probably discover you inhale and exhale at a different rate. The faster partner can try breathing more slowly, and the slower partner can speed up. Keep doing this until you can reliably and comfortably move through the exercise at the same rate together.

Exercise: The Twin Serpents

For this practice you must seal the centers and draw the circle around yourself and your partner. Begin with yourself, seeing and feeling the serpent's rise as your pleasure and excitement increase. When you climax, place the energy again in the globe above the head.

You can aid your partner as well by visualizing the serpent's rise in their central column as they become more excited, and especially during climax, when they're most likely to lose concentration on the visualization and feeling.

Try also placing your right hand at the base of your partner's spine and your left hand at the base of the neck. Remember, the right hand directs and the left hand attracts energy; when you place your hands along the spine, you set up a circuit of your own energy, which helps to stabilize and direct your partner's energy rise.

Exercise: The Shared Central Column

Sitting or lying face to face in lovemaking, see and feel the central column as shared, just as you visualized and sensed the shared centers. With rising excitement, note the rise of the serpent in the channel. Place your hands on one another's spines to aid the flow, and place the energy of climax in the shared globe above the head.

Effects of the Serpent's Rise

The goal of the exercise is to maintain a steady rising of energy from genitals to crown whenever you make love.

As the subtle body begins to respond to the increased energy, you'll notice a series of effects that might be called psychic awakenings. They correspond to the energizing of each center, the development of the senses of the subtle body.

First, of course, the genital center releases its energy. If you think of the power of sexuality as a snake biting its own tail--the infinity sign--this occurs when the snake releases its tail.

The visualization may sharpen, and the sensation of energy increase in heat, solidity, and rate of rise. You might find yourself seeing bits of color or movement at the edge of your eyes.

Early emotional effects can bring unresolved conflicts to the surface, or uncover buried memories. You might find yourself reevaluating your sexuality, becoming more assertive about what you like and don't like, or experimenting new behaviors you hadn't been inspired to try before.

Whenever the energy level surpasses your comfort level you can call a time out. Ground the circle, sit on the ground with your feet stretched out, and touch the ground. Sitting on the ground brings the base center in contact with or closer to the earth, and stretching your feet out separates the feet centers from the rest of the body, aiding them in their natural energy slowing effect. All these movements help to wick off the excess energy.

The subtle body pyrotechnics increase with the awakening of the navel center; we might call this set of experiences the smoke of the rising fire. You may begin to see your own aura or your partner's, as balls or shimmering halos of color. You might see the circle around you, or see geometric shapes as you become visually aware of the subtle body and the other worlds. You might begin to sense energy movements you're not consciously generating in your partner's body and aura or in your own.

You might feel or see your subtle body merge with your partner's. Sitting or lying face to face, you might notice the centers along the central column suddenly merge or "blow open".

If you don't remember your dreams, you may now. Your dreams might also change, become more vivid, bring up unresolved issues in your emotional life, center on archetypal symbols, suggest steps you can take to improve your life on any level.

If the dreams become frightening, stop working with the rising energy and practice dreamwork. You might also pick up the discipline if your dreams become vivid or the symbols change radically; it can help you understand the messages and actualize the suggestions.

The awakening of the heart center generates beginning flickers of awareness of the touch of Spirit. You may find that you have insights into your own nature, magick, and the world. You and your partner might begin to speak to one another in new voices, the voices of your higher intuition.

The throat center's awakening produces the steady conviction that you are divine, that your partner is divine, and that you are loved by divinity.

When the rising energy awakens the third eye center we move into the realm of the cloudless sky, direct experience of the world of the divine.

These are generalizations. Your own experience may differ from this, and you might not understand what's happened until you've had a chance to assimilate the event. Also, the centers won't open all at once. The whole process can take many years of a lifetime to complete, or it can happen very quickly, depending on the previous emotional and magical work you've done and how rapidly you can assimilate the influx of energy and sensation.

What's important is to stay comfortable with the process, to cool down and work on grounding and balance if you find it's gotten too hot to handle, and to accept who you are.

Your partner might pace your development, or you might have very different experiences at different times. It's important too to accept who your partner is, and to understand that both experiences are valid.

Chapter Six: Manifesting Results, Touching the Divine

As lovers we seek to bring greater pleasure, affection, assurance, and devotion to ourselves and to our partners. We dedicate ourselves to achieving health, emotional security, magical knowledge, and skill, in order to bring these as gifts to those dearest to us, and in order to gift ourselves with a well-lived life.

As magicians we understand we can direct the unleashed energy of the body to craft swift and effective changes in our physical lives and our hearts, and to directly experience divinity without and within.

No one of these things has a higher value than any of the others. Each depends on the other: we must maintain health to continue to make love with others and ourselves; we must generate a stable and happy home to be free to concentrate on experience of the sacred; and touching the divine forms the central focus of our lives, without which life in the body, the home, the friends and lovers have no meaning.

What is important is maintaining the balance. To be effective we must be able to generate any of the results possible with sex magick, and to know when to concentrate on each of them.

Creating Change

All the subtle body exercises strengthen general health. You might discover you can move through your day more quickly, sleep fewer hours, and accomplish more tasks with the energy available.

Exercise: Healing the Body

Sexual energy can be specifically directed to increase strength and comfort in the body. The technique is the same for acute problems--pain in a muscle, a broken limb--and chronic ones: tension in a part of the body, a weak organ, a recurring headache. Immediately before, during if possible, and just after climax, see and feel the white or golden light moving along the spine and out to the affected part.

If your partner has the problem, place your hands on the weak part of the body. Visualize and sense the energy of both your own climax and your partner's climax to that part, surrounding and strengthening it.

In addition to focusing directly on a single point, sexual energy can be spread throughout the whole of the body. Again just before, preferably during, and just after climax, visualize and sense the flash of energy moving up along the spine, out through the trunk of the body, along the arms and legs, and into the neck and head. This works both in making love with yourself, and in helping to heal your partner. That power refreshes the exhausted frame and accelerates the recovery from illness.

Exercise: Manifesting Abundance

Sex magick can help us to lead the kinds of lives we dream of. Do you need an income or a better place to live? Is there a particular thing that would increase your freedom and your enjoyment of the world? Make a simple image of the thing you need. Imagine yourself when you've accomplished what you want--what do you look like? How do you feel?

Make love with yourself or your partner. Direct the climax energy to the crown center, placing the image there at the same moment. Let yourself feel as you will when the change you've willed happens in your life. Then immediately release the image and the feeling. If you're working with a partner, you must both agree on the goal, and the technique works best if you share the image and feeling.

Record the working in your journal. When the item enters your life, record that as well.

Exercise: Transforming the Heart

Hetaera training works toward clearing the pain of past traumas, establishing gentle and honest communication, building self-confidence, and a sense of personal power.

Sexual energy can accelerate a specific change you're working on as well. In the section on containing energy we examined blocks in the subtle body centers and their emotional effects. Now, you can direct climax energy at the center you're working with, or at a center your partner seeks to balance. Imagine and feel the energy surrounding the center, gently illuminating and heating the center as it gradually opens.

Create an affirmation that expresses the change you want to make in yourself and how you see yourself:

> *I love myself. I am filled with peace. I am an effective (business person, musician, communicator, therapist, etc). I express my anger out loud, calmly, and effectively. I acknowledge and appreciate my own beauty and the beauty around me.*

Repeat those affirmations to yourself as you make love with yourself, and immediately after climax. Your partner, if you are working with one, can give you those affirmations immediately after climax as well.

Imagine how you will look and sound and feel when the change has occurred. Place that image in the crown center when you direct sexual energy there.

Exercise: The Magical Child

Sex magick redirects the energy designed for procreation in order to manifest what we want to bring into our lives. However women who wish to conceive can use sex magick to help achieve that end. In this case you will be working with the natural energy of the body, using conscious energy work to overcome blockages and barriers to conception and create a positive energy current to bring a new being into existence.

You and your partner together can create an affirmation welcoming a child:

> *May our love bring a new life into our lives to share our lives.*

Partners can guide the energy of the working directly into the womb, mixing the energy of both partners to create the foundation for the reception of the divine spark that will animate the child's life.

Women can continue to use sex magick throughout pregnancy, to bolster their own health and that of the child's.

The Divine Without and Within

How do you perceive divinity? Where does the divine force reside? Look like? How have you related to deity in your life? In hetaera time, write a journal entry about these questions.

Find or draw a picture which expresses your understanding of the divine force. It could be an image of the earth or a galaxy, wind moving in trees or a rose, a particular deity, or a snake.

You can set up a small table in your hetaera space and place the image on it. Meditating on the image focuses our understanding of the sacred and its place in our lives.

Exercise: Making Love with Divinity

However we understand, name, see, know divinity, sexuality provides the most intimate form of worship.

In making love with yourself, dedicate your pleasure to the Spirit. At climax, place the image of deity at the crown center, and open yourself to the sense of presence.

The image may simply form and fade. You may find that the image moves; the Spirit may reach to touch you, or speak to you, or a feeling may sweep your senses. Accept whatever occurs with as open a heart as you are able, and allow yourself to express, in words, aloud or silently, or by simple emotion, your response to the Spirit.

In working with a partner, both of you must agree that you will dedicate this particular session to worship of the divine. You don't have to use the same image, and you may not have the same experience of response even if you do. Take a few minutes to lie in each other's arms, and share what you have seen and felt. Remember that each of you takes equal love from the divine, increasing your ability to love one another.

Exercise: You Are Divine

Remember that each of you is a unique expression of that divine force as well, and can embody an image and experience of the sacred for one another. Speak affirmations aloud to one another at the beginning of your lovemaking session and throughout it:

> You are sacred. Your body is a temple of divine force. The Spirit's light shines in you.

Brandy Williams

Remind yourself as you touch your partner that you are touching divinity, that these genitals which can create another human being represent the force which creates all life.

After climax, lie in one another's arms, and give yourselves time to talk to each other and share the experience. Remember, you are listening to the words of the divine force; here most especially, the Voice of the Spirit may speak through the throat of the lover.

Not every lovemaking session, either with yourself or with a partner, must be devoted to achieving a particular end. Even when you choose to contain and channel sexual energy, you may simply store it in the crown center for use at a later time. When you do choose to begin to reach for one of these ends, it's wisest to eventually perform all the workings to maintain the balance of body, heart, mind, and spiritual aspiration.

Love is limitless. Why limit the goals you can achieve with the power of love?

Chapter Seven: The White Marriage

The serpent rises, awakening us to a life of love.

The opening of the senses signals more than the simple joy of a new lover. The serpent's first touch especially wakens the subtle body to life in the world of ecstasy. That warm glow of golden joy trains the eye: to the brilliance and subtlety of hue and tone and texture; to the glimpse of divinity on every face. Every human face reflects the divine, and the Snake coils in every dancing movement. How sharp our perception of the lover's call! How acutely we note every glance, the curve of the neck, the drape of the hand, the inviting tilt of a hip, the flutter of collarbones with every breath, like wings.

Breath is life. Breath is song, our call to rejoice in the life of the beloved body, that of our lovers' and our own. The moans of pleasure phrase our lovers' music. The sounds of the world shape the moan of love, and every bird call, the mournful note of a flute, the strum of strings in a chord, the sighing of wind strikes the heart with agonizing tenderness. The flash of amber light opens every pore to the honey-flow of touch. Even the sensation of wind, water, sun on the skin comes welcome, surrendered as we are to the awareness of the pulse, the power of blood and bone. Animals we are and grateful for it, for every breath and every flavor of food, binding us inextricably to the web of life as we bind ourselves, body and body, to love.

The world opens out and we are the world: the dance of shadows on the ceiling, the sway of trees outside the window, the layered sound upon sound falling on the ears, the rippled texture of the bed. The world contracts and we are the lover's body, love itself: the shadows in an eye looking out upon infinity, the minute variations in the breath, the feathery touch on skin so gentle and exquisite we can almost feel the fingertip whorls.

The colors swarm and shivering spirals sweep the body. Electric blue vortexes, clouds of glittering white, rainbow halos surround us. The hand touches the lover's thigh and disappears, melts, forehead presses to forehead soft as a tissue to silk. The Voice speaks, saying: I have always been here, I will always be here, you can never lose me, you have always known me, take this comfort, let me exalt you, follow me to the place you have forgotten you have always known. Then we can begin to learn about love.

Marriage means commitment. The White Marriage ritual demands a total commitment to pleasure on all levels, for a single night. We bring together all the skills we've learned and the changes we've made to form a single, formal dedication to sacred sexuality. A clean and healthy body, a clear heart, a calm mind, and an open, soaring spirit unite to create a moment of transcendence, working through the physical body to achieve awareness of the highest divine nature.

Marriage means celebration, and this ritual includes a feast, offered to a partner or offered to divinity. The simple act of sharing food makes the union concrete, honoring our bodies and our connection to the world, symbolizing the nourishment that intimacy brings us, acknowledging the spirit that flows in every living thing.

Marriage brings permanent change, marking a milestone in life. The White Marriage dedicates us to treating every sexual experience as a sacred act. Once we perform this ritual we can never again treat touch as casual or approach pleasure with guilt or reluctance. We are both free to fully express and enjoy sensuality, and required to remember that our bodies are temples for the most divine force.

It's equally effective to work with yourself alone, or with a partner if you have one. Partners may choose to do the rite alone first--that makes channeling and visualizing easier. In that case you may choose to perform the ritual again with your partner.

The first step in any ritual is preparation, and the most important thing to prepare is yourself. Before you perform the rite, make certain you're ready to bring your whole attention to it. Ask yourself these questions.

Prepare Yourself

Take a moment to clearly state to yourself or to your partner your reasons for undertaking this step. Are you working on releasing old fears and guilt around sexuality? Are you motivated by a desire to embrace your own sensual nature more completely? Are you eager to express your growing love for your partner, or you own joyfully expanding self?

Then all systems are go it's time to prepare yourself. Take a shower or bath and pamper yourself with all the things you like, like your favorite soap or bubble bath. You've explored changing your physical appearance; this is the time to wear the make-up, jewelry and perfume or cologne that brings you the greatest sense of self-confidence, of being attractive and lovable.

Wear white clothes. A simple method is to invest in a length of white cloth and wrap it around yourself, tying it off with a white scarf. The important thing is to choose clothing that makes you feel special, and that feels good against your skin.

Prepare the Space

Make a physical space ready as well. You can perform the rite on a bed, or arrange cushions on a floor. If you have white sheets you can use those as well.

Set a small table near the bed and lay a white cloth on it. Place on the table: a white candle; a plate or tray containing white foods; a glass or goblet containing a white or clear liquid; any oils or incense you decide to use; the image you've chosen to represent your understanding of the Divine Spirit.

In extended lovemaking sessions, it's a good idea to have foods close by, easy finger snacks that raise the blood sugar level quickly. Then you don't have to jump up to raid the refrigerator!

Ritual foods also remind us of our connection with the earth. They should include a grain; a dairy product; a meat or vegetable; and a fruit or sweet. The grain represents the centering power of the earth; a meat reminds us of our kinship with all living things, and our mortality; the dairy product provides a nurturing and calming effect; and the fruit or sweet represents excitement and passion, generating emotional as well as physical energy.

Here are some examples of white foods:
Meat: fish, chicken. Vegetarians can choose cauliflower and potatoes.
Grain: rice, white bread.
Dairy: milk, white cheese, yogurt.
Sweets: peeled bananas, apples, pears, white chocolate, vanilla ice cream.
Liquids: milk, white wine, lemonade, seltzer.

You might arrange the foods on a tray or a white plate; they'll become an offering to the Divine Spirit, and to the divinity within your partner.

You'll spend some time with the rite, and will want make sure you won't be interrupted. Unplug the phone, put a do not disturb sign on the door, make sure all the doors and windows are locked. Couples with children may choose to hire a babysitter for an undisturbed night. Just before you begin the marriage, check to make sure you have everything you'll need.

The rite includes dedications to make to yourself, your partner if you're working together, and to Spirit. You can copy them on a sheet of paper or index cards and read them aloud; you can memorize them; or you can make up your own words for each step of the rite while you're doing it.

Dedication

When everything has been prepared, you're ready to begin. If you're working alone, light the candle on the table, and say:

--I dedicate my body as a temple for the Divine Spirit.

--I dedicate the pleasure of my body to my own acceptance of my self-worth.

--I dedicate the joy of my heart to my increasing joy in life.

--I dedicate my knowledge and skill to my expanding ability to act in the world.

--For this night I pledge my commitment to the union of body, pleasure, joy and skill.

--May this experience bring me an awareness of the Divine Spirit, without me and within me, now and forever.

Partners sit facing each other and say:

--I dedicate my body as a temple for the Divine Spirit.

--I dedicate the pleasure of my body to your pleasure.

--I dedicate the joy of my heart to your joy and our joy in life.

--I dedicate my knowledge and skill to our expanding ability to understand each other.

--For this night I pledge my commitment to the union of our bodies, in pleasure, with joy --and skill.

--May this experience bring us an awareness of the Divine Spirit, without us and within us, now and forever.

Sealing Centers

Those working alone next seal themselves, touching each center. With each touch repeat:

My body is a sacred temple of the Divine Spirit.

Couples seal one another's centers, saying:

Your body is a temple of the Divine Spirit.

Make the circle around yourself, or around yourself and your partner.

Touch the top of your head and say:
I am a child of the earth. I am human, and express the divine in my ecstasy. So too I am a child of the stars, and a vessel of the most sacred Spirit. May I be touched by the union of the divine.

Partners touch one another's heads and say:
You are a child of the earth. You are human, and express the divine in your ecstasy. So too are you a child of the stars, and a vessel of the most sacred Spirit. May we be touched by the union of the divine.

Now hold your hands over the plate and cup, saying:
This food and drink is of the earth as my body is of the earth. This food and drink contains a spark of the Divine Spirit as I contain the Divine Spirit. As these substances combine within me, may I be nourished in my quest for awareness of the Divine Spirit.

Those working alone can dedicate each morsel to the Divine Spirit, saying:
You nourish me.

Both partners can repeat the dedication, and then feed one another, saying:
May you be nourished.

The Marriage

Couples may find the process of feeding one another flows naturally into caressing. If you're working alone this is the time to make love with yourself, with joy and acceptance, using whatever sensual items you have discovered please you most. Use all the skills you've built through previous exercises, circulating energy with visualizations and breath control.

At the moment of climax visualize and feel energy rising up the body's central column to the globe above the head. As the pleasure fades from intense sensation to warm afterglow, allow an image of the Divine Spirit to form in the globe.

Couples may seek to experience the Divine Spirit in each other. You may see flashes of color around one another's eyes, head, shoulders, or have an internal sensation of touching a sacred being. Again, freely express the emotions you experience at that contact. "You are divine, my love."

When you, or you and your partner, have released the energy of the working, allow yourself to relax for a while in the certain knowledge that you are divine and loved by divinity.

Closing

When you feel ready to return to normal consciousness, thank your partner and the Divine Spirit for the experience. Saying a short acknowledgement brings the rite and its commitment to a formal ending, signaling the seriousness of the act and providing a transition to everyday life.

If alone, say to yourself:
This union is complete. May I be ever nourished by my contact with the Divine Spirit.

Say to your partner:
Our union is complete. May you be ever nourished by your contact with the Divine Spirit, and may your memory of our touch be ever sweet.

Blow out the candle.

You may choose to move directly into sleep at that point and complete the closing in the morning. Or you may choose to clean your space before going to sleep. Put the items on the altar away, change into other clothes, reconnect the phone. Remember to make notes on the rite in your journal as soon as possible, while the details are fresh.

You may choose to repeat the rite to increase your contact with the Divine Spirit. You may also choose to perform the ritual specifically to strengthen your health or manifest a change in your life. Rewrite the dedications to suit the purpose of the working and your personal taste.

Ritual Outline

Here's an outline version of the rite:
- --Self check/partner check
- --Define intention of working
- --Set up space, table and meal
- --Bathe and clothe yourself
- --Make sure you won't be disturbed
- --Recite dedication
- --Seal and circle
- --Dedicate food
- --Consume meal
- --Build energy
- --Release energy toward intended result
- --Reabsorb energy
- --Thank partner/divinity
- --Grounding:
- --Clean space and table
- --Record the working

The snake of pleasure rises within the body, lifting head to the crown center, the blossoming flower of union, a burst of flame. The touch of that flame transforms us: we are fully human, and more than human. We have looked out upon infinity and drifted in an eternity of love; and we return to our waking lives with the knowledge that we will never be alone again.

Section Two: Red Hetaera

Chapter One: Magical Sexuality

I stand amid the crags of the mountain, tucked away in a clearing of the tangled forest. Cedar and hemlock trunks ring me round, and no living thing moves or calls in the gathering darkness. With reverence and love I have bid farewell to the setting sun; now I await the moonrise.

When the first crescent lips over the edge of a nearby peak, I take up the knife to draw the circle. I pick up the wand then, standing back from the altar, within the shield and lens of the gate between worlds to lift up my voice: "Behold the candidate! I offer myself: youth, never touched and trembling; wanton, accepting and giving every conceivable touch; initiator, granting ecstasy. I invoke you! Come to me!"

And the power responds.

We've defined a hetaera as one who approaches sexuality with a healthy body, a clear heart, and open to the touch of the divine. To truly work within a magical framework we must sharpen our minds, the fourth foundation of our system. Hetaeras acquire the knowledge of the power of touch.

First, we broaden our understanding of the physical body, comprehending and increasing control of climax. This increases our capacity for pleasure, and our choices about when and how to release the energy of a working.

Next, we delve more deeply into the structure of the subtle body. Energy loops within the aura, circulating constantly; we study that movement in order to direct it, building the amount and kind of energy funneled into the central channel.

We focus on discipline, lengthening the time between arousal and climax, raising sexual energy and sending it; and creating a magical personality, a set of characteristics we pledge to maintain during workings. Discipline is the magician's essential characteristic; it grants control of a working, builds trust in ourselves, and generates the safety that handling intense energy requires.

Anyone who has completed the white hetaera exercises can work through the red hetaera set as well. The ideas and skills we learn here form part of a common occult heritage for all Western magical systems.

Those who already have some magical experience will encounter some familiar ideas presented in a new light. We can use magical skills in a specifically sexual way--harnessing sexual energy for use in any kind of ritual structure.

This section, however, is by no means an in-depth study of magick, just a particular application. True freedom and power require the open-minded study of several magical systems. The magician's first task is to read widely and with dedication. Learn to cast a circle and to understand the Tree of Life, the Qabbalah. Pick up at least one text on history, psychology, and mythology. Most importantly, understand that no one book or teacher has a chokehold on truth; there are many points of view on any given subject. As we trust first and foremost our own experience, so we must learn to form our own opinions.

Most especially we turn critical thought toward two of the processes considered here in depth: polarity, and alchemy.

Many magical systems stress the primacy of polarity. It's a habit of thought: split physical phenomenon into two categories and then relate the items in each of the categories. Male, female; hot, cold; day, night; sun, moon; active, passive.

To demonstrate the point: there are positive and negative aspects to polarity. At its worst, it supports a justification for limiting behavior--other people's and our own. What is female is also cold, night, moon, passive; what is male is hot, day, sun, active. Some who follow this line of thought assert that women must never take active part in a working. Others accept this as a given, but go on to assert that all of us must balance masculine and feminine characteristics within ourselves. For example, women must balance their "natural" tendency toward cold, passive behavior.

The tension between opposites undeniably generates tremendous amounts of energy. We will consider various kinds of poles that don't tie a set of characteristics to men or women, and examine techniques for working with that tension outside the gender-specific context. Anyone, alone or with any kind of partner, can take advantage of polarity energy.

Alchemy relates to polarity but isn't identical with it; the science of transmutation separates and recombines. The hetaera's alchemy centers on charging and using body fluids, the natural elixirs generated by our work.

Our alchemy also deals with the transformations we undergo as we worship divinity in order to realize ourselves as divine. As dedicated hetaeras we turn our attention to specific deities, adoring them in order to comprehend the world, our place in it, and our own divine natures more deeply.

We call the power, and the power answers; and in that answer, we hear the echo of our own voices, the whispered exchanges of lovers who seek not to dominate or to submit, but tease and surrender--to unite with that which we adore.

Chapter Two: The Sexual Persona

As our skill in generating and handling energy increases, we naturally begin to work with more intense types and amounts of energy. Our practice sessions become more psychologically demanding, which is both riskier and more satisfying. We can affect changes in our personalities and in our world quickly--sometimes more quickly than we can handle comfortably.

Magicians build safety mechanisms allowing us to handle large amounts of energy and changes in consciousness. The most important of these is the magical personality. The personality serves as a receptacle for energy and a tool to develop magical skill. It forms a barrier against too sudden a change in who we are, a distancing device allowing us the time to assimilate the result of a magical working.

It's called a personality because it's a layer of consciousness built around the normal waking self. We become that person only when we do magical work.

Each of us is many people, depending on where we are and who we're with. The office worker in a suit, the laborer in overalls, the cook in an apron, changes personality substantially playing with the kids or walking in the park with a lover. Magicians become aware of this process and take conscious control of it.

Actors change personalities onstage; a magical working is a kind of stage, both requiring us to move and speak and act with discipline, and allowing us to play with new characteristics and experiences. Actors have at least a skeleton of a character to work with. The suit, the office, the expectations of coworkers clue us to the behavior expected of us--in fact, many books and workshops offer training in taking on a professional persona.

Rules for building a magical personality are less clear-cut. We don't have a script to follow and we don't have the example of many people around us to emulate. We can, however, use some of the same techniques that let us build other kinds of personas.

First, we separate the personality from our daily selves. This person is who we are when we practice sex magick, and only then.

Even those who already have a magical personality will want to build a new one specifically for this purpose. You're going to be a different person in a sex magick working than in a circle, coven, lodge, or temple. You'll use different tools--primarily those of your own body. These workings rest on their own structure and tend to generate intense amounts and types of energy. You'll probably find you hold yourself differently, talk differently, and experience different sensations than those in your other ritual workings. It's most flexible and most effective to dedicate a personality to this type of working alone.

The first step in building a magical personality is choosing a new name. This name augments the sense of separation from the daylight personality. Pick one that gives you a sense of being sensual, powerful, and capable. You might pick up an unusual name book, page through mythologies for names of human attendants of divinity, look up famous hetaera's names and stories in encyclopedias, or choose the name of a flower or a tree or a celestial body.

Next, buy or make a garment especially for use in hetaera time. Natural fabrics feel most comfortable against the skin and drape most gracefully. Silk especially not only looks and feels sensual, but acts as an insulator protecting the subtle body against energy loss. It should be either white or red in color. As with the white marriage clothing, you can simply buy a length of cloth, cut a hole for your head, and tied it off with a scarf. You can buy a pattern and sew a flowing robe. Some lingerie stores, too, carry gowns and suits with suitable cuts and fabrics. You can also simply use the garment you wore for the white marriage.

The important thing, again, is to be comfortable wearing the garment, and to feel that it flatters you. Keep it separate from your other clothing and wash it by hand. You must never wear it for any other purpose than hetaera time exercises and workings, and it's a good idea always to wear it when you put on your personality.

Jewelry helps build the hetaera outfit. Arm bracelets, necklaces--especially solidly built chokers--earrings, hip belts, ankle chains, and rings are all appropriate. Start with a single piece; you can add to it as you develop a sense of your new self. Lovers can also gift one another with items for a set. Experiment with the associations of various metals and semi-precious stones. Which most effectively express the personality you're creating?

You may have experimented with perfume, cologne or oils when you changed your appearance. Oils especially carry their own kind of energy, helping to create a ritual mood. Try different kinds: floral, rose and jasmine; spicy, sandlewood and patchouli; aromatics, like musk. Some stores carry sample racks that buyers can dab on to try before buying. You might pick several and mix them to create your own signature fragrance.

Building the Personality

Personalities carry behaviors. Workers are expected to be punctual, to suppress anger and dissatisfaction, to be cheerful and polite. Parents cultivate patience, firmness, and nurturance.

Hetaeras share some characteristics with magicians in general: discipline, concentration, precision, enthusiasm, and the ability to keep silent about a working and its results. In addition we cultivate those qualities which make for good lovers: attention to the body's responses and to our partner's needs, and the ability to be vulnerable and gentle with our partner's self-revelations.

What's your image of the perfect lover? Describe those characteristics in your journal. With these guides, make a list of the behaviors you want to build into the personality.

It's most helpful to choose characteristics that balance your outer personality. Do you bring great concentration to bear on the details of your life? You might choose to add spontaneity or humor to your list of hetaera behaviors.

What would you look like if you had those characteristics? How would you hold yourself, what likeness would you project? In hetaera time, visualize yourself, standing or sitting, looking as you would if you knew these things were true.

Exercise: Assuming the Personality

In hetaera time, put on your garment and dab oil on your centers. Put the piece of jewelry you've chosen on, saying as you do your new name. Say aloud, "I am," and read the list of characteristics you've generated. Standing or sitting, close your eyes and create the image of yourself as you'd appear with those characteristics. Open your eyes and stretch. Take the jewelry off and say your birth name. Set your garment aside.

Repeat this exercise for a week in hetaera time. You can add this to other exercises you're doing. From now on, always assume the magical personality for your hetaera practice.

You don't have to assume the personality every time you make love with yourself or your partner. You might find that as the power available to you increases, you prefer to keep at least your jewelry handy to keep the option open. In working seriously with particular divinities, using the personality will be a requirement.

Working with Others

You can choose to enter into this process with a partner, sharing the experience of choosing clothing and oils and constructing your characteristic list. This can augment your sense of trust in one another, helping to ensure the personalities' compatibility.

You can also each build the personality separately, introducing yourselves to each other at the end of the week and revealing your new names. Then you have a chance to learn about a whole new person, the personality your partner has chosen. It's a private choice; both are equally effective.

Chapter Three : Building and Circulating Energy

The human body is capable of experiencing a great deal more pleasure than most of us allow ourselves to feel. Expanding our capacity for pleasure can be an end in itself--after all, pleasure is part of the reason we practice this form of magick!

As magicians we gain control over the physical mechanism of climax, increasing the time we can spend in making love and the intensity of the sensation. With greater control and increased time in lovemaking sessions, we circulate energy through more channels in the subtle body, building to a more intense release both of physical pleasure and of the energy of the working. Handling larger amounts of energy increases our effectiveness in achieving the results we want from the working.

Exercise: Increasing Physical Pleasure

Climax releases the blood built up in the genitals during sexual excitement, and tends to release the energy built up in a working as well. Postponing climax and experiencing more than one climax help us retain and add to the energy we're generating. For men this means learning to climax without ejaculating, and for women to experience a form of multiple climaxes.

A climax without ejaculation can be fully as intense as that with ejaculation. The penis contracts, and at times can give off a bit of ejaculate or a clear fluid (like that bit of lubrication generated with the first erection).

It's easiest to experiment first in making love with yourself. Bring yourself right to the edge of climax, and then stop stimulation and breathe deeply. You can also press the spot between the base of the penis and the anus for a second or two. Then continue stimulation. Don't worry if you go over the edge; focus on the feeling you get just before ejaculating, and try to stop next time when you get that feeling.

Many men report having this experience while making love. Practicing helps bring the ability under conscious control. After a few weeks or months you'll be able to sustain an erection for hours at a time and to ejaculate only when you consciously choose the experience.

Women can experience a similar sensation; we might call it climax without contraction. Again, the physical burst of pleasure can be fully as intense as the climax we've been taught to expect. The vagina contracts only slightly, and in the lower part of the canal. In an end-climax, the vagina closes and opens rapidly like a fist, and the upper part of the canal expands with a ballooning effect probably designed to draw sperm nearer the cervix (the opening to the womb).

The exercise for learning the skill is almost the same. Make love with yourself, bringing yourself to the edge of climax, and then stop stimulation and breathe deeply. Then continue the stimulation.

In both cases the physical effect is to continue to store blood in the genital tissues--the penis, or the web of tissue in the female pelvis. Climax with ejaculation for men or with a full set of contractions for women releases the stored blood, requiring a longer buildup before another climax can occur. Multiple climaxes allow sexual activity to continue at a fully aroused level.

From now on in this book the word "climax" will mean this partial-release kind, and "end climax" will mean that with ejaculation or a complete set of vaginal contractions.

Working with Others

When you've gained some skill with these techniques, you can try them out with your partner. When you feel a climax approaching, stop movement and immediately communicate this to your partner. You may want to choose a safeword. The safeword is a signal for both of you to stop what you are doing immediately. It can be any word you choose, "time out" or "blue", or you can just use the word "safeword." This prevents misunderstanding, especially if you use words like "stop" or "don't" or "no" in a playful or teasing way.

It's vital that you stop what you're doing immediately when your partner uses the safeword. Violating that rule even once can seriously damage the trust you require in moving to more intimate and vulnerable communication with each other, and in giving control of a working to one another's hands.

You can aid your partner during the two or three second break by breathing deeply, by not speaking, and by remaining still. Then you can resume your lovemaking. If one or both of you loses control and experiences a full climax, you can build your trust in one another by being gentle. This isn't a contest or a proving ground--it's a way to enhance your union. There's always next time!

Exercise: Climax Along the Centers

Controlling climax allows full control of energy rising in the body's central column, especially when used with breathing patterns.

Try this the next time you make love with yourself in hetaera time. Stimulate yourself, holding a breathing pattern, to a climax, imagining and sensing energy rising from the genitals to the heart center. Make the next climax an end-session type and visualize and feel the energy rising to the globe above the head.

You can direct the energy to each center in turn with each climax. See and feel the white or golden light moving from the genitals to the navel center with the first climax. With the next, direct the energy from the navel center to the solar plexus. Continue with each climax pushing the built-up energy to the heart, throat and forehead centers, and then again release the energy with an end-climax, sending the energy to the globe above the head.

The effect of this working is enhanced when you visualize each of the centers with its appropriate color and symbol.

Working with Others

The Western ideal is that couples will climax together. Of course this rarely occurs, and can even get in the way of energy movement in a working. When both partners are experiencing multiple climaxes, it's almost impossible!

However, you can move energy from center to center with a partner. Use any face to face position, and see and feel the centers in both your central columns merging, so that you share the same centers. With your first climax, visualize and feel the energy moving from the genital to the navel center. See and sense the energy moving again from the genital to the navel center with your partner's climax.

With multiple climaxes especially, it can be difficult to know exactly when your partner has crested. You might want to set up a code word to let your partner know what's happened. You can say, "now," or "next", or the name of the center you've just pushed energy up toward: "navel".

When both of you have said "navel," you can take your second climax, seeing and feeling energy moving to the solar plexus center, and then saying "plexus".

If one of you gets ahead of the other, taking climaxes more quickly, it's not a problem. Just pause at the forehead center to let your partner catch up before you both release the energy with an end climax.

This can be a complicated working, and again, if you lose control during the process and crest or spill, contracting and ejaculating, before the completion of the visualization, just try again in another session.

With your partner's permission, you can also visualize the energy moving upward through the centers in your own central column only, without coordinating that movement with your partner's energy rise. The important thing is to remember to send the energy to the globe above the head at the completion of the working.

The Side Channels

The subtle body circulates energy in more channels than we've discussed so far. The energy we take in with every breath flows into two tributary channels bracketing the central channel. They begin in the region of the genitals and twist around the central column, ending at each nostril. As you practice moving energy through the subtle body, they gradually untwist so that they run in straight lines on either side of the central column.

Many poles have been assigned to these tributaries: male and female, hot and cold, night and day, sun and moon, fire and water; red and blue, red and white, gold and silver...You can give the tributaries any attributes you like. In general, the channel to the right side of the central column is considered male, solar, hot, red, day, etc., while the left channel is female, lunar, cold, blue, night, and so on.

In hetaera time, establish a rhythmic breathing pattern. As you inhale, visualize and sense energy running in the side channels, from the nostrils in a straight line to the genitals. As you exhale, see and feel the energy funnel into the central column, moving upward to the globe above the head.

You can choose to see the energy in the side channels in any colors you like. Try the visualization again the next time you make love with yourself.

Brandy Williams

Working with Others

In your next hetaera time together, sit comfortably on your heels or with crossed legs facing each other, just as you did when you practiced other breathing meditations.

Watch your partner's breathing rate and listen for the inhalation and exhalation. As your partner breathes in, visualize energy moving from their nostrils down the side columns to the genitals. As your partner breathes out, see the energy move from the genital center to the globe above the head.

You can use this visualization/sensation technique to add energy to the working during your lovemaking sessions.

The Circle Channels

Two circuits in the subtle body move energy along the spine and the front of the body. In a healthy subtle body during most activities, energy flows from the genital region upward to the bottom of the mouth, and from the roof of the mouth to the forehead and then down the spine back to the genitals.

In hetaera time, see and feel these circuits connecting to move energy in a circle. When you've visualized your first complete circle, imagine that energy moving back up into the central column.

Now reverse the flow of energy. Imagine and feel the light moving from the mouth down the torso, through the genitals, up along the spine, over the top of the head to the mouth again. Make love with yourself; sending energy in both directions along the circle, and then into the central column.

Do you note a difference in the directions? Many report a sensation of coolness and a slowing of arousal when energy moves in the waking-time pattern, up the torso and down the spine. Reversing that flow tends to speed up and heat up the energy in the working.

That's a rule of thumb generally true for all subtle body channels. You might have noticed that the Accepting Spirit exercise directed energy from the head to the feet, downward, while most of the sexual visualization/sensation techniques end with energy moving from the genitals to the head, upward. In general, sexual magick reverses the flows of energy in the subtle body and channels all energy flows in the body into the central column. This acts immediately to clear blocks, to strengthen the subtle body, and to increase the amount, heat, and speed of the energy in the working.

Working with Others

Just as partners can share a central channel and sealed centers merge when torsos press together, the side and circle channels merge and intertwine during lovemaking.

When you place your genitals against your partner's, and the two of you lean your foreheads together, the circle channels connect and intertwine. Imagine and feel the white or golden light moving down your partner's back, into your body through your genitals, up your torso through the mouth to your forehead, and out to your partner's forehead again. When a circuit is completed, return to seeing and feeling the central column, moving the energy up to the globe above the head.

Now repeat the pattern, reversing the flow of energy. Imagine and sense energy moving down your partner's torso, through the genitals, up along your spine, and through your forehead back to your partner's torso. When you've completed the circuit, see and feel the energy moving back up the central column.

If your partner is working on climax control, you can use the first visualization/sensation technique to slow down their response, and the second to speed up their movement toward climax.

Oral sex positions allow for the development of several kinds of energy movement techniques. If you're devoting yourself to worshiping your partner, bringing your mouth to your partner's genitals while he or she relaxes and surrenders to the experience, you can see and feel energy moving straight up your partner's central channel. You can increase the energy of the working by visualizing energy moving into the side channels when your partner inhales and up the central column on the exhalation, and by imagining energy moving in the circle channel.

Those options are available if you're engaging in mutual oral sex. There the circle channels function somewhat differently. Visualize and sense energy moving from your mouth through your partner's genitals, up your partner's spine, up over the head through your partner's mouth back to your genitals.

When you've gotten this far you have a choice. You can simplify the circuit and the visualization and simply see the energy moving back up your own spine. Or you can see and sense the

Brandy Williams

energy moving up your torso back to your mouth. In this case reversing the flow of energy and imagining the energy moving down the spine or down the torso will fairly seriously slow the pace of arousal, and may even ground the energy out altogether.

Pathways

Minor channels spread out from the main channels throughout the auric field. In general they run from the central column out--along the arms and legs, for example. You can use the energy moving out along the limbs in making love with yourself, and in directing energy to your partner through your hands.

Breathing rhythmically, imagine and sense energy moving up the central column to the globe above the head. On the next inhalation, draw some of that energy down to the heart center and then out along the hand. You can add to the energy available by directing breath down the side channels and into the central column, or by concentrating on the circle channel for a few moments.

If you're stimulating your own or your partner's genitals, you can imagine and feel the energy moving from your hand through the genitals directly up the central column. You can also place your hands along the side channels, as for example at the breasts. See and feel the energy moving down the side channels and then again into the central channel.

Try placing your hands at your partner's feet during lovemaking. This traps the energy that normally moves out the soles, and can add considerably to the energy available. That is--it can be a thrill!

Energy also flows directionally in the subtle body, from the left hand, foot and eye to the right. In general, the left side of the body accepts energy, while the right side gives it off or directs it. When you're facing your partner, energy passes automatically from your partner's right eye to your left. Paying a bit of conscious attention to that process can help to augment it.

Stimulating the Centers

Placing water, oil or body fluids at the major and minor centers helps focus energy at those points. If you're working to clear a block or to heal a particular part of the body, you can try dabbing a bit of healing oil (say, aloe vera) on the affected part. Try licking your hands and

85

placing them on your partner's nipples. That can generate a gratifying response!

Cosmetics can function to pool energy at a minor center--for example, rubbing kohl on the eyes. It's possible to find kohl at India import stores. You can also use washable body paints to draw designs on the skin. You could, for example, paint symbols at each of the centers--a silver crescent at the navel, an upright red triangle at the heart, and so on.

Stones placed along the centers serve both to concentrate energy on the spot, and to direct a particular energy to the center. In hetaera time, try laying on your back on a comfortable surface. Place a moonstone or crystal at the navel center, a warm red stone like carnelian or garnet at the heart center, a blue stone like turquoise or lapis at the throat, a purple stone like amethyst at the forehead. Practice the energy rising visualizations and sensations, either as visualizations or while you're making love with yourself.

You can have the stones set in jewelry--the moonstone or crystal in a hip belt, the warm stone on a long necklace to reach to the chest center, the blue stone in a choker, the purple in a head circlet.

Applying the Techniques

Reading through a list of techniques such as this, it's possible to torture ourselves with feelings of inadequacy. Can I be a real hetaera if I don't string five visualizations together and have ten climaxes in a row?

Of course you can! All of these are options, allowing solo workers and partners to generate more energy and direct it specifically through the subtle body. These techniques can be useful; however, the only real necessity is to direct energy into the central column. Remember the first rule of magick: if it works, use it; if it doesn't, drop it. There's no need to complicate your practice with a distracting level of concentration.

There aren't any shoulds in sex magick, just choices. What matters most is that you are happy and your partner is happy with whatever you do. What could be more important?

Chapter Four: Adoring the Divine

Each of us has our own understanding, image and experience with divinity. We can, however, learn from those cultures around the world and in history which have venerated gods and goddesses of love.

Focusing on a particular god or goddess allows us to generate a specific image, and to contact the energy or force of that deity. The goddess or god will have attributions--color, time of day and of year, animal forms--that allow us to build particular rituals in their honor. Each hetaera must choose the god or goddess or pair who most attracts us. It's a mutual process; the deity must choose us as well!

The goddesses and gods come to us in their own way, bringing each of us an individual understanding of who they are. One way to look at them is that each of them has two aspects: a mature, powerful, fulfilled form, and a younger self. We can think of the Youthful aspects as sister and brother of the god and goddess, as the foremost of the followers in their train, as the god and goddess themselves when they first wake to awareness of being.

The Goddess

The ancient cultures surrounding the Mediterranean associated goddesses of love and sex with the planet Venus. As the morning star the goddess is the Maiden, goddess of the dawn, glistening with the first light, decked with ornaments of red-gold to trip lightly through the day's course, bringing a smile and a graceful touch to every heart at every moment. Her names include Eos, Awsos, Ushas, goddess of the dawn; Persephone, the reborn Maiden of spring; Hebe, Flora, and Kore, the eternal Maiden.

As the evening star she is the lover, proudly displaying her body and her beauty, bearing the knowledge of her experience, the certainty she is adored. These are the most famous of goddesses, Aphrodite, Hathor, Inanna, Asherah.

Maiden

She who waits
She who hunts without hunting
She who will never be touched and not touch
She who returns to the womb of her mother
the cave and the earth to seek silence and dark
in the night, in the winter, the maze of the heart
to renew her lone power, pledge love to herself
and arise white and new from the earth again
She who courses the sky in the change of the moon
who is crescent and disk, who is sickle and bowl
turning back to herself
She is ever herself.

The Maiden waits.

She has waited for a long, long time. She is the hunter who bides with patience for the creature to move.

Hers is the first realm we must visit, the wild hills, the places humans have never gone, where the wild nut drops its fruit and the wild deer flashes between the trees. Hers are the first questions we must answer in unlocking the secret soul within the body.

Who are you when you are alone?

Solitude is the mirror she hands us and we must look without flinching. The mirror reads back to us who we are when we walk the forested hills alone with only ourselves for companions.

Can you be companion to yourself?

She calls us, who will not give of herself, to give ourselves to our own love, our own destiny. She will not allow us to un-know what we discover here, what sometimes it is convenient to forget, painful to remember: our safety, our beauty, our integrity depend on giving ourselves first what we need of ourselves, and never giving this away to another.

Can you defend your integrity?

She Who Slays will loose a silver arrow for us if we ever deny ourselves again. She lays the weapons in our hands, the bow, the feathered shaft. Running in her band we develop the muscled body, the strengthened heart we require for the moment of necessary denial.

Can you follow the rhythm?

She points to the changing of the moon, swinging through the sky from crescent to globe, sickle to dark bowl and back to the crescent that is her bow. All of us, man and woman pulse to that tide, the ebb and flow in the water and blood. We are born, we grow, we are fulfilled, we are slain, we are cleansed, we are born again, with every course of the moon.

Will you dare the descent?

She it is, too, who stands at the mouth of the cave, the door of the maze, the realm of the serpent of the earth, beckoning us to enter, to withdraw from all we have known, downward, inward, to the heart of the darkness, feeling our way along slick stone walls until we can hear the heartbeat of the Earth. We must face the demons there and slay them-look them in the eye and know them, and own them. These are our own fears, our own sorrows, our own pain, and each and every one of them is our own choice. Choose again or make different choices, make and unmake and remake who we are.

Do you trust yourself?

Hers is the thread we clutch that leads us back again, hers is the torch borne far ahead, beckoning us to a new birth. We must hold to the thread of that faith in ourselves, we must cleave to the knowledge of the goal or our work.

Dare you rise again?

When earth has covered the mouth of the cave, hers is the voice in the world beyond, urging us to dig and push and claw our way through. Hers are the hands awaiting to pull us when it seems our strength has deserted us. Hers is the grace that rescues us when we have gone as far as we can go, hers is the healing that wraps the cloth around our bruised body and swaddles the wounded heart.

Are you ready to risk yourself in love again?

When we emerge from the realm of the Earth Serpent, the walls of the labyrinth itself, hers is the web struck by the first light of day. She it is who leads us down to the sea, to wash the soil from our skin. We rise in the dawn, bathed in the rosy light and the morning dew, wrapped in the mist the Lady of Love throws around us.

Can you release me?

We seek the Maiden in ourselves. We find her face in every woman. We trace her pulse in every man. She is the wild heart and the hidden wisdom with whom we begin and to whom we must return, again and again, for renewal.

Prayer to the Maiden

Maiden of the Wild Heart,
you who are yourself to yourself,
teach me to love myself.

Warrior Inviolate,
you who no one ever touches,
help me stay true to myself.

Warrior Implacable,
you who slay those who defile,
lend me strength and shield me now.

Guide of the Hidden Maze,
you who hold the thread of knowledge,
show me where my true path lies.

Maiden who is Ever-New,
you who course all changes whole,
help me birth myself again.

The Goddess as Lover

Hers is the call to open the heart: to ourselves and that grace of forgiveness for our own faults, to love that within us we would cast out and cut off, the dark and the light equally. She calls us to the abandon of physical pleasure, gesturing to us to touch ourselves, love ourselves, and lose ourselves in the sheer joy of living.

Hers is the call to open the heart: to the beloved other, loving the flaw along with the virtue, the body as well as the mind, to surrender to sensation and the delight of the senses, to move to the lover's heartbeat and breathe the lover's breath.

She calls us to adorn ourselves, with oil and paint and color and silk and gold to render ourselves desirable, lovely and handsome. To pose with the poise of the confident: am I not loved? and do I not love? and what more is there to life than this?

Her touch it is that turns our head to watch the lover's eyes, to ache in the lover's absence and rejoice in the lover's presence, to rest our eyes savoringly on every movement, to treasure every moment in the beloved's favor as the goddess' own gift.

She challenges us to abandon our boundaries, to give ourselves to union. She has no patience with the needs of solitude; she unbinds us from our separate lives and binds us again to the life of another.

She it is whose womb quickens with life, whose touch opens our wombs. Just as we give ourselves to our loves, so our bodies and our lives stretch to encompass the life of another. In the cycle of life and death she stands as the eternal gateway, opening us to possibility, to sacrifice and joy, pain and fulfillment, in the generation and renewal of human life itself.

Her lessons are those of the sea, of flow and of ebb, of love and the lack of love. We can ride the tide of emotion, acknowledging our humanity, drenched in the sweet and the salt of life's waters and nonetheless steering our own course; or we can resist her pull, and in the struggle drown in the overwhelming currents of fate.

We can gulp in as air the bracken splash of sorrow, bitter with loss and regretting each withdrawn touch. Or we can sip that measure that falls to us, secure in her promise that the tide will always change, and she will always rise again with the dawn, draped in rose and scented with rose and calling us again to the pulse and joy of loving.

She is the lover: the one who we love, the one who we become when we love.

Prayer to the Goddess Lover

Lady of Light and Love
help me to open my heart
as the dawn breaks every day anew.

Lady of Light and Love
help me to express passion
as the noon sun blazes endlessly.

Lady of Light and Love
help me to be compassionate
as the evening shadows soften the world.

Lady of Light and Love
guide me as I guide others
open me as the gate of life

Lady of Light and Love
help me to love wisely
as the night brings endings and new beginnings.

The God

Just as the goddess of love has a young and a mature side, the god of love comes to us as a youth and as a man. In his boy form he is Aphrodite's winged son Eros; as Attis, the rising green shoot of the spring; as Adonis, Ganymede, Hyakinthos; as all the young gods of Egypt, Horus and Khons; as Kouros, the eternal youth. As a full grown god he comes to us with power as well as joy, the god of the erect phallus, Pan, Dionysus, Dumuzi, Min.

Youth

He who is the beauty of Youth
the son of the earth, the Maiden's brother
He who delights in the swift athlete games
who pits muscle to muscle, who guides the thrown ball
He who delights in the craft of an art
in tripping of flute and of harp and of voice
is the one who beckons through the swinging door
the guide on the road, on the bridge, on the journey
is the one who speaks through smoke and image
to limn what may pass, what has passed, what will be
wielder of the sword that cuts the part from the whole
bringer of death, of insight, of dreams,
reminder of that which blooms briefly in life
looking out at the world
knows himself for himself.

The Youth appears. When the time for the change comes he stands before us with the reminder of the necessity: it is time to leave, it is time to return, it is time to withdraw, it is time to move out into the world again.

We may resist him, we may ignore him, turn away and pretend we never saw him; then he comes as trickster, the mischievous elf running ahead of us in the forest, calling "follow me to a place of beauty!" and disappearing just before we encounter the impassible cliff, allowing us to make the discovery that we must trace a longer and more difficult trail to safety.

If we accept, if we welcome him, then he stands beside us as guide, holder of the light, the comforting hand ready to help us cross the threshold.

Quicksilver light at the edge of vision, he calls to us to the life of the senses. He cries, "Come aware! come alive! use your eyes and your ears and the bone and blood given you to participate in being." He is that which focuses on sounds in the environment; on the feeling of air against the skin, the sensation of feet against earth, the swing of arms as we walk along, the pulse of the heart together with the evenness of breath. He is the sight when it settles on the particular, moves beyond the blur of green tree to note the myriads of single leaves on the branch.

He is the pride of the body and the discipline of its training, the count of the exercise, the differentiated muscle. He is the armor that settles beneath the skin when we must move through the workday world, the suppleness of motion when we glide on the dance floor, the strength when we give ourselves to running along the sea; the warrior readiness.

His is the snapping moment when drowsiness becomes sleep, when the door closes or opens, when what is hidden is revealed, when the dreamer wakes. The first shoot from the seed in the spring, the sudden wind of a still hot day, the flash of a bird here-and-gone mark his presence.

He gifts us with the attentive ear of the student, the measured cadence of the teacher's voice. He brings along with change the knowledge of the change--seek him in the throw of the cards, the toss of the stones, the voice of the oracle. Seek him too in the shifting otherworld of dreams, in the single image that makes the meaning clear.

His is the clarity that makes distinctions--it is this or it is that. The grey mist is rain or it is fog. The sky lights with city haze or the wash of clustered stars. The water is very cold or very hot. The sound is a car's cough or gunfire.

When we are in danger his is the shove in the back toward survival: keep moving through the snow, keep running from the attack, pick yourself up when hope has entirely deserted and put the next foot in front of the last. Do it again. Do it as long as it takes.

At life's end too he comes to us to herald and ease the transition, let us know when the time has come to end the struggle, to drop the load, to stand and face the death that awaits us. He will be firm if we resist him, kind if we accept him then, but he will come.

We may experience him as harsh or gentle--it's all the same to him; what matters to him is the movement itself. We see him in the firm body of youth, man or woman. We find him in the joy of the moment when an inspiration opens new understandings. Our lovers find him in comprehending suddenly a new aspect of us.

Prayer to the Youth

Flower of awakened spring,
you who triumph over winter,
help me make this start again.

Warrior of discipline,
you who hold fast to a task
help me stay along this course.

Oracle of things to come,
you who mark a lifetime's changes,
show me what will come to pass.

Guardian of boundaries,
you who frame the door and threshold,
help me make this limit now.

Youthful patron of my art,
you who grant the gift of grace,
favor me with inspiration.

Dreamtime guide through smoke and wonder
you who hold the guardian's lamp,
help me find my way again.

The God as Lover

The pounding of the drum is the stamping of the hoof
the call in the wild woods to come and dance
the lifted hand leading us to the couch
the frank gaze meeting our eyes with a challenge:
do you dare? Can you face me?

94

Can you face what I awaken within you?
It is the call to the pleasure of the flesh
the recognition of our animal nature
that once embraced leads us to the deepest spiritual truth.

As all gods do this god holds power. His however is not the power of the gods of war, the gods of dominion, who take by force and keep by might. Rather, his is the power to win with joy. He invites without requiring, courts without compelling, affirming connection and life.

This god is the god of strength, of muscle and sinew, of the pulsing of blood. His is the compassionate touch of the healer, the infusion of vigor which renews the flagging body. He comes to us, in solitude, in dreams, consoling us, releasing the knots of tension and pain which bind us, freeing us to move, freeing us to love.

His strength is that of protection. He is brother and father, the one who stands with us when we most need support, whose voice is the voice who answers our loneliest call.

As lover he seduces with the sheer joy of the body, beckoning us to feast on the sweet fruit of the earth, to revel in the touch of silk against the skin, to sink into the yielding cushions and yield ourselves, opening as the blossom to sun, relaxing in the warmth of his touch. Then in the moment of our yielding we know his strength, our soft relaxation meeting the formidable stone of his vigor, the implacable rising of pleasure.

His strength is the potency of embodiment. When the Goddess Lover opens the womb, his is the touch that quickens, life catching fire from life.

He is the lover: the one who we love, the one we become when we love.

Prayer to the Lover God

Lord of Light and Love
help me find my strength
in courage and understanding.

Lord of Light and Love
stand with me in my need
that I may be sustained.

Lord of Light and Love

release me from my pain
that I may be renewed.

Lord of Light and Love
bring to me new life
that I may bring to life.

Lord of Light and Love
help me to love freely
that I may know life's joy.

The Lovers

The world's stories speak of the moments when Goddess and God turn to love. There are the male and female pairs: Inanna and her honey-man Dumuzi; flute-playing Krishna and milkmaid Radha; Aphrodite and her youthful lover Attis; Eurynome and Ophion creating the world.

The male-male pairs are less well known but can be found. Greek vases show Apollo flying in the clouds with his young lover Hyakinthos.

Even more rare are the female-female pairs. As Apollo loved Hyakinthos, Aphrodite must have loved Peitho; and Artemis ran with her sacred band of women.

It falls to us to seek out these stories, and to write new stories of our own, honoring the love of the gods for the gods, and the gods for humans, and humans for the gods.

Exercise: Devotional to Deity

Although these are general understandings of the deities of love, each magician can learn by seeking specific deities to understand, honor, and embody. Search references and examine images until you find a form which you can wholeheartedly reverence. Those who already worship a goddess or god can simply include those deities in sexual working.

In working with goddesses and gods, our first step is to study them. Read all the material you can find on who worshiped them, who their people were, where they lived, in what time periods. What are their myths? What colors, animals, celestial bodies are they identified with? See if you can find pictures of statues or carvings of your deity.

Begin with an encyclopedia. If you live near a university library, you can look the name of your deity up in the catalog. The first book you find will refer you to others. Sometimes just reading a general history of the people who worshipped them leads to valuable clues.

It's especially important to pay attention to the gifts they like to receive. Did the people who worshipped them before you bring a particular kind of stone, oil, or food to them?

If the stone or food is difficult to find in your region, search out a similar item from your own area of the world. How does your part of the world differ from the place the deity was originally worshipped? For example, many of the goddesses associated with sacred sexuality are portrayed as riding lions; their temples were decorated with lions. Is there a cat-like creature (say, a cougar) in your ecosystem? Place an image of that creature, the cougar for example, near the image of your deity.

Exercise: Adorations

Ritual invites the deities into our lives. Set up a shelf or table in your room or hetaera space dedicated to your chosen deities. Find or make an image of the deity and place it on the table.

Light a candle or burn a bit of incense, and speak aloud one of the prayers to the Youth or the Maiden, or to the lover goddess or god.

As you move through your day, search for images or feelings or events that remind you of the god and goddess. For example, every day as you see the sun for the first time you can make a prayer to the Maiden.

The god or goddess you're researching may have been especially honored at a particular time of year, or there may have been several celebrations throughout the year for their worship. What was happening in that country at that time of year? Were they honored at planting time or harvest? Make a celebration at planting or harvest for your area. Adapt your worship of your deity to your own area.

Exercise: Dedications

The ritual becomes more formal as we dedicate ourselves to the worship of our chosen deity.

Dedications to the Maiden and Youth are white workings. First, make a journal entry about what they mean to you, what you hope they will bring to your life, how you plan to worship them.

Choose a day near the new moon for the rite. Women can also choose the day after your menstruation ceases. Place a white cloth on the table that holds your image of them, and decorate it with a white candle, flowers, stones, shells, feathers. Prepare a white meal and place it on the table as well.

Take a long bath, meditating on renewal and beginnings. Dress in your white clothing, and anoint yourself with a lightly scented oil. Assume your magical personality.

Sit in front of the shrine you've created, light the candle, burn a lightly scented incense. Say the prayers to the Maiden and Youth, and read your journal entry aloud as your dedication to their worship. Eat part of the white meal, offering the rest to the god and goddess; return the rest to the earth or a running body of water.

Dedications to the Lovers are red workings. Repeat the rite with red materials, using a richer scent for oils and incense. This time, seal and circle yourself and make love with yourself, dedicating your pleasure to the god or goddess.

Chapter Five: Polarity: The Dynamic Tension of Life

I worship at the altar of your body. Lover, you are my tools: your mouth my chalice; your hands, the disc; your tongue, a knife; and where we are joined is incense, smoke and flame, my love. We rise.

They say you are the sun and I the moon, my love, that I reflect your light; but when we rise together, we shine we equal brilliance, mirror our shared pleasure with even joy.

They say you initiate, my love, and I must be willing, receptive. But ah! your smile when I take the power to act, and you surrender!

They say I am a gate, my love, and my one touch renders you sacred. Then who will open the gates of love for me to flood me clean?

They say we are different, love. That I give what you need. I can give without limit and you must conserve. And they lie.

When I breathe in your mouth, inhale your breath, slipping in and out of your soul, when I slip my soul in and out of you, the power is the same. When I am flame and you burn and shake with the heat of our sealed souls, sweet lover, you know. The power is the same.

Most discussions of sexual ritual eventually confront the issue of polarity. The basic idea is that an energy of attraction pulses between two opposites, and that by bringing opposites together we make a whole.

The most obvious opposites or poles that present themselves for use in sex magick are male and female, man and woman. The attraction between the sexes is, of course, a powerful form of energy. However, gender polarity can trap us in an either/or kind of thinking that excludes some people from some kinds of power.

Either you're male or you're female. That can be used to mean, for example, either you have male, solar, fiery energy or female, lunar, watery energy. The argument can be extended to set characteristics and behaviors in concrete, and to assign a greater value or flexibility to one of the poles. If you're a woman you must always generate lunar energy, and therefore must always be passive in a working. In practice this sometimes means that entire energy-working systems are set up for the benefit of heterosexual male magicians.

One western writer not too many years ago suggested, for instance, that the male practitioner find a female partner who isn't too bright, keep her in the dark about what he was doing, erase awareness of her identity as an individual and imagine her instead as the incarnation of his particular goddess. This was intended to unite his masculine being with the essence of femininity and thus lead him toward a mystical understanding of the universe. What's in it for the woman, and how denying participation and humanity to one of the participants in a sex magick working generates transcendent consciousness is left to us to puzzle out.

Another writer offered the opinion that women have unlimited amounts of energy while male bodies generate finite amounts, and therefore women can make love with each other while men sin against nature to do so. In fairness, eastern Tantric texts are often written within similar value systems, and many western writers simply follow their lead.

Our physical gender does not determine the type or amount of energy we have access to, and does not determine the roles we must play in sex magick workings. Polarity magick need not be based in gender--the world offers many pairs of phenomena and ideas. Same sex couples and solo workers as well as heterosexual couples can take advantage of the energy of tension between opposites, and the unity can and should benefit both partners equally.

Polarity Workings for One Person

Physics provides us with one modern mystical theorem. The universal material, the stuff of world and cosmos, we call energy. We perceive energy as being composed of waves and particles--as being static, or moving.

The human body can represent the interplay of those forces, of matter and motion. The body itself represents form, while the power of sexuality we unleash with our magick is force--energy in movement. Try meditating on that the next time you make love with yourself. You can give yourself affirmations:

> My body is form, my body is earth; my pleasure is force, my pleasure is spirit.

When we visualize and sense deity in the globe above the head, we set up a human/divine polarity, offering our mortal pleasure as a gift to the gods. In hetaera time, seal yourself, saying "I dedicate my body as a temple to the worship of Aphrodite" or "Dionysus". Then make love with yourself, imagining the god or goddess in the crown center, saying, "Aphrodite," or "Dionysus, I give you my joy that it may please you."

Energy moves between poles, pulsing in a beat. Our feet contact the force of the earth, while we draw sunlight and moonlight through the crown center. In hetaera time, visualize and sense white light moving from the crown center to the feet for the space of one breath. In the next breath, see and feel golden energy moving up from the earth through the feet to the crown center. You can use this exercise to build energy as you offer your pleasure to your chosen divinity.

Polarity Workings for Couples

Partners can choose to enact roles based on poles other than male and female. The most immediately powerful pair of opposites is active and receptive.

The active partner can direct both the physical movements and the circulation of energy throughout the session, while the receptive partner focuses strictly on enjoyment, the pleasure of the moment, willing and joyful surrender to the active partner's direction.

Here there are two crucial rules. The first is: discuss the working first. This can be an excellent opportunity to experiment with new lovemaking techniques. If one partner particularly likes an activity the other doesn't, both of you may decide to include that behavior here, as a gift from one partner to the other. However, it's not a requirement! The receptive partner must draw limits, and the parameters of what's acceptable and what's not must be understood in advance. This is a license to play, not to genuinely dominate.

The safeword for stopping the session can come in handy here. If either one of you finds comfort levels have been crossed, you can call a time out using the safeword. Then you can move out into trust space to establish guidelines more firmly.

The second crucial rule is: change roles. In the beginning it's a good idea to swap roles every other working. If one of you plays an active role in a working, you should take a receptive role in the very next session. This allows for equal development of both partners, maintains a balanced relationship, and builds trust. It allows you to share a set of similar experiences--you'll both be aware of the special problems and joys of each of the roles. Switching roles also builds the polarity beat, the movement of energy between the poles.

These rules hold good for every kind of polarity working.

You might enjoy structuring a fantasy around the role playing. The active partner can be an Eastern prince and the receptive partner a concubine (female) or catamite (male). The receptive partner can be a troubadour, and the active partner the lady who commands him absolutely; or the lady can seduce her serving maid.

The fantasy frame can help both partners enter freely into the spirit of the working, and can also mark it out more sharply in your minds: this is a play, a special activity, which adds to but does not supplant other kinds of workings.

Psychological frames such as these can unearth serious issues around control and surrender. One or both partners can discover or confront fears around loss of control, or secret desires to be in control or surrender absolutely. It's also possible that one or both of you will recover a memory of past abuse.

These techniques, being powerful, must be handled carefully, after some trust has been built between partners. If one of you becomes uncomfortable with the working you must shut it down immediately, and neither of you should ever pressure the other to enter into a polarity session. As always, if you discover any trauma that affects your attitudes toward sexuality, you should immediately seek healing--see a therapist and draw on the support of your partner and your friends. If your partner uncovers a previously unexplored trauma, you can build tremendous trust and bonding by supporting whatever actions he or she takes to deal with it.

On the other hand, role playing can help to balance and heal the effects of past experiences. Women or men who have been passive in relationships, accepting the direction of their past partners, can grow in assertiveness and confidence by taking an active role in a polarity working. Those who have been accustomed to being in control have the opportunity to discover the joy of releasing responsibility and constant conscious awareness of what's going on, and simply enjoy the moment of pleasure and trust.

You may also find that you deeply enjoy enacting one of the roles, while the other takes some effort. That's a normal human characteristic. As magicians it's essential that we train ourselves to be capable of taking on any role. As individuals, it's important to recognize the preferences that make up our unique character.

These workings, being powerful, should also be used sparingly. You might want to engage in two polarity sessions in a row (to give both partners a chance to enact each pole), and then to focus on other kinds of workings for at least two sessions.

There are other pairs you can enact which don't depend on taking or giving up control of a working. They include: sun and moon, sky and earth, hot and cold, water and fire, older and younger. Each of the pairs represents a type of energy, a state of consciousness, a set of behaviors and movements. You can choose to enact each of them separately, or to link them: sky and fire are hot, while earth and water are cool.

As you become more aware of energy movements in a working, you might note differences in those movements from moment to moment and working and working. The differences center on speed, temperature, texture, color and heat. Sky or air energies are light in color and temperature. Fire energy is heavier, brighter, and generates the most heat. Water energy is cooler, moving more slowly and darker still in color, while earth energy is heaviest. Decide which half of the pair each of you will enact. Then choose clothing, jewelry, and colors which reflect those characteristics.

Begin the session, as always, by assuming the magical personality. You can seal your partner using affirmations which reflect the poles he or she has chosen to embody: "I dedicate your body as a temple to the night-blooming flower, the cool and delicate inspiration of the moon." Or, "Your body is a temple of the sun, the blazing fire of passion." Throughout the working, use body movements and voices which reflect those roles.

Whether you are working alone or with a partner, when the working is completed, affirm that the energies brought together have combined within you or within both of you. "I am fire and water, air and earth. You are warm and cool, light and solid, sun and moon, in control and surrendered. We are bright and dark, old as time and born again in this moment. We are body and spirit, human and divine, all opposites are made one within us. We are united, we are union itself."

All things are made whole in love.

Chapter Six: Magical Discipline

Discipline means having knowledge and using it, training ourselves to increase control of the energy in a working. It means being good at what we do and expanding our sexual and magical abilities.

It doesn't mean forcing ourselves to do things that repulse us, or tying up our partner in a working! It means choosing the moment we release the energy of a working with skillful control of its direction toward a clearly articulated result.

Exercises that build magical discipline involve learning to hold back from releasing pleasure for long periods, and inducing climax without physical stimulation, alone and with a partner. The techniques increase the intensity and quantity of energy available during workings, improving the practitioner's control of that energy.

Working Alone

Exercise: I Enjoy Touch

Even those of us who embrace pleasure wholeheartedly can benefit from occasional periods of experimentation. The next exercise works to stretch the amount of time and the ways in which we accept pleasure. It also works to disconnect the act of lovemaking from the pressure to achieve an immediate goal, focusing us on the sheer joy of touch.

In hetaera time for two weeks, and in that period of time, don't masturbate. You may choose to make love with a partner, or you may choose to pay attention just to yourself for now.

You can return to your normal patterns for a period of time, or move directly into the next step. Repeat the exercise, this time including the genitals--but don't climax. Do this for two weeks as well.

When you've worked/played through these exercises, try them again, this time masturbating to climax. Make a deal with yourself: the next time you feel the urge to make love with yourself, do it. You may retire to the bathroom in your home or workplace; you may be walking in the woods; you may be having a conversation with a friend; wherever the mood strikes you, excuse yourself for a few minutes and bring yourself pleasure.

Working with a Partner

Exercise: Sharing Sensual Exploration

Couples fall into lovemaking patterns: when, where, sequence of positions or behavior. Exploring varieties of touch with one another can break the patterns, renewing your interest in one another and teaching each other by example what each of you enjoys.

As you try out new types of textures and touch in making love with yourself, you can try them out with your partner. Stroke one another with silk and stones. Touch and tickle and kiss the toes, the ears, the backs of knees. Stroke any part of each other's skins but your genitals.

Do this for two weeks without bringing each other to climax. Then you can take a break, or move directly into the second exercise. Repeat the sensual exploration, this time touching each other's genitals, but again not bringing each other to climax, again for two weeks.

Exercise: The Untouchable Lover

This is another fantasy role-playing technique. Imagine yourself as a Lord or a Lady, while your partner is a servant attempting to win your affections. You can become a prisoner unfairly held in a foreign land and a visiting. Perhaps you are young lovers in a parlor, with both your parents watching your conversation but unable to overhear your words. For some reason they want to keep you apart, or you do not wish to reveal your love to them.

The situation allows you to see and speak to one another, but not to physically touch each other or to be explicitly seductive. Can you arouse one another without attracting the attention of your retinue, the guards, your parents? Can you conceal your rising passion from them? You can experience whatever level of pleasure you are comfortable with, including climax and end-climax, but you must not physically touch one another.

Continue the fantasy for a week, not making love with yourself or each other during that time. You might even choose to sleep separately for the duration of the working. At the end of that time you can arrange to meet in a safe place, and bring the working to a close with an end-climax for both of you.

If you are working without a partner you can simply imagine your partner. You could act out the fantasy in a public place to heighten the sense of reality and danger.

Exercise: Irresistible Pleasure

Can you make yourself to climax without actually touching yourself? Can you bring your partner to climax without actually physically touching your partner's body?

You can do anything you can imagine to yourself or one another short of physical touch: wear anything, say anything, move any way. How close can you bring your hand to your partner without contacting skin? How seductive can you become, to your partner, to yourself? Stroke your skin or your partner's skin with a silk scarf. Read an erotic poem. Slowly consume a piece of fruit, or feed one to your partner. Use every technique you can think of to so deepen the trance of pleasure that an end-climax is inevitable.

Exercise: Mirror Workings

The next time you make love with yourself in hetaera time, imagine another self stepping out from your body, either of the same or opposite sex. Make love with your lover/self, and imagine and feel them making love with you. At the end of the session, imagine that self stepping back into your own body.

Have you ever watched yourself during lovemaking? Try it alone in your hetaera space. Let the mirror reflect your face, your genitals, especially any part of yourself you haven't looked at before. Can you watch yourself climax?

Partners can make love before the mirror. If you normally keep your eyes closed or make love in darkness, you can light candles, watch each other's faces and genitals, mirror one another's movements. Can you look in your partner's eyes when you climax?

All these exercises broaden the context and extend workings for a longer period of time. Long term tension workings constitute a powerful polarity magick; the poles here are withholding and release of energy and climax.

Remember to put on the magical personality at the beginning of the working, channel energy into the central column, and record the results.

Chapter Seven : The Body's Natural Alchemy

Alchemy means changing a substance into something different--using a physical vehicle to carry the touch of the divine. In a sense, all sex magick is a form of alchemy, as we work through our bodies to the mystic experience of union.

In sex magick, alchemy refers specifically to several processes: charging physical substances with particular kinds of energy, combining energies of two bodies, and combining body fluids and consuming them to absorb and transmute their energy.

The body naturally transforms physical substances into energy. Food, water, and air change character when we consume them, generating the power that allows us to move through our days and our lives.

We take advantage of the body's alchemy when we dedicate foods for ritual use. The things we eat and drink in sexual ritual are set aside, made sacred or special, partly by their color. The blessing we say over the foods charges them with energy as well. White foods can be charged with moon, water, cool, night energies, while red foods can act as vessels for sun, fire, hot, daytime forces. As you hold your hands over the plate and cup and speak the prayer, visualize and feel white or red light flowing from your hands to the foods.

When we bless ritual food and drink and consume them during a working, they not only sustain our physical bodies, but the energies they contain help to build the subtle body as well. As you eat and drink the charged foods, visualize and sense white or red light expanding outward from the abdomen to vitalize the whole subtle body.

Sex magick workings automatically charge body fluids. However skilled we become at channeling energy upward along the central column, the physical body and subtle body both give off energy through the genitals at an end-climax. That's why genital lubrication, menstrual blood and semen in particular take on the energy of a session. Of course, the whole physical body and the whole subtle body participate in sexuality, and so other physical secretions--saliva, tears, perspiration--take on the charge of a working as well.

Brandy Williams

Sex magicians have for centuries combined body fluids and used them in a variety of ways. Western sex magick has in the past laid heavy emphasis on combining semen with menstrual fluid. This substance forms the sacrament of many a published ritual. It's been considered so important that entire systems focus largely on this technique.

However, AIDS and other sexual diseases pass through unprotected sexual contact and contact with body fluids. Many people have become permanently sick or have died through unprotected sexual contact. Sex magicians are not invulnerable to disease. Magick will not save us. Protecting ourselves will.

Educating ourselves about safe sex is the top priority for any sex magician. We can use condoms, oral sex barriers, spermicide, and alternatives to genital contact, to protect ourselves against contact. Any sexually active magician also needs to be tested for sexual diseases, including but not limited to AIDS.

Fluid bonding, choosing to share fluids with a partner, is a very serious step. It requires honesty on the part of all partners, not just about past encounters, but about all encounters in the present. It also requires testing until all partners are sure they are safe before beginning the fluid bond.

Although fluids do carry the charge of the magical working, they are not essential to sharing energy. Those who are not fluid bonded need not expose themselves to uncertain contact. Instead, partners can become consciously aware of the energy of the working, and visualize their separate energies combining and then being re-absorbed by each of the partners.

Because body fluids take on the energy of a working there are techniques that involve retaining the fluids. Semen in particular has been considered to be so laden with the energy of a working that eastern and some modern western texts advise ejaculating seldom or never. Some texts include instructions for reabsorbing the physical fluid through the mouth of the penis.

Body fluids do, indeed, carry tremendous charges. This is just as true, however, of menstrual blood as it is for semen. Women are equally likely to lose the energy of a working through shedding menstrual blood as men are through ejaculation. This energy loss is mitigated through energy awareness and the use of techniques such as sealing and circling. Women may choose to share menstrual energy with partners or may choose to wait to do a working until after their menstrual period ends in order to preserve energy. It depends on the woman's health and individual choice.

Working Alone

Exercise: Experimenting with the Body's Alchemy

When we are making love with ourselves, we can experiment with combining body fluids. One of the best and briefest summaries of alchemy is "solve et coagule"--separate and combine. When we combine two body fluids we increase the amount and types of energy the new substance contains. Consuming those fluids again allows us to reabsorb the energy of a working.

Those working alone can, for example, combine genital fluids with saliva. Touch your finger to your mouth, then to your genitals. Close your eyes for a moment to visualize and feel the two fluids mixing. Bring your finger back to your mouth and taste the new fluid. See and sense the energy from the fluid moving into the central column and expanding out to the whole subtle body. Try mixing perspiration and tears with saliva, lubrication, semen or menstrual blood as well.

If you've been making love with yourself as a form of offering your pleasure to divinity, you can treat saliva or tears as being infused with the presence of your deity and your genital fluids as containing the essence of your passion. Mix and consume them as a symbol of your union.

The combined fluids can also be used to consecrate a physical object. Mix them in the oil you use to anoint yourself, dab a bit on your jewelry or on the plate and cup you use for your ritual foods. You can also dab a bit of the fluid on the ritual meal or dip a finger into your cup to endow the food and drink with a special charge.

Working with Others

Exercise: Absorbing the Energy of a Sexual Working

After a working, lie quietly with your partner. See and sense the energy both of you have expended. Feel these energies combine. Now re-absorb this combined energy, through your genital center, up into the central column, and spreading throughout your entire body. You can also recirculate this energy through your partner's body by seeing and sensing the energy movement within your partner.

Fluid-bonded partners can mix genital lubrication, saliva, semen, menstrual blood in any possible combination. Touch your partner's genitals and your own to mix the fluids, and then feed them to your partner.

Depending on your sexual preferences, fluids may already have been mixed at the end of a session. Saliva mixes with genital lubrication in oral sex; semen mixes with genital lubrication or menstrual blood in heterosexual union; semen mixes with anal liquids in anal sex. If that's true, simply touch the area where the fluids have mixed, taste them and share them with your partner.

Partners who have been enacting roles can consider their body fluids as carrying the energy they've been representing. When you combine your physical secretions, or visualize and sense their mixture, you bring together the force of sun and moon or fire and water. Taking in the energy of the combined fluids ends the working with a symbol of their unity.

Whether the energies in the working are absorbed physically by the participants or are absorbed in a pure energy form, mixing energies is a form of polarity work, and can form a satisfying conclusion to a working.

Chapter Eight: Becoming Divine

The power comes and does what it will, possessing, easily, this willing body, demanding the full sweet measure of my passion.

Ah. I recognize you.

And in that passion a rising as of fire: a supple twining round all the limbs, the swaying lift of a hissing mouth: the Snake comes to my skillful summons.

I am Deity's plaything, transformed by their pleasure, drawn out building, cresting--and returned to my own body in the lingering ambiance of exaltation, consciousness flashing into regions much finer than it could reach on its own, their gift.

The hetaera's path works through physical pleasure to worship the divine, to court the touch of the divine. The ultimate aim of our worship is to unite with that which we adore. We can worship divinity within our partner; we can join with the divine in our own bodies.

Working Alone

Exercise: The Divine Lover

Those working alone can approach deity as a devotee, uniting with the goddess or god in sexual embrace.

Set up your hetaera space just as you would if you were entertaining a lover. Bathe and dress yourself. Lay out a ritual meal. Pay special attention to your altar, putting new incense out, using new candles.

Assume the magical personality. Seal and circle yourself, and include the altar in your personal circle. Then invoke the deity-- Aphrodite, Dionysus, the Maiden or Youth, or your personally chosen divinity--using the prayers given in this book or those you've found or created for yourself.

Now eat some of the meal, laying part of it aside for the deity. Address the Lord or Lady, telling them what they mean in your lives and what it means to you to love them.

Make love with yourself, visualizing and sensing the god or goddess making love with you. Bring yourself to an end-climax, dedicating your pleasure to your divine lover.

Finish the meal, remembering again to leave part for your lover. Thank the Lord or Lady for the presence. Close down the circle. Give the food back to the earth by burying it or tossing it in a body of water. Record the working in your journal.

Exercise: Taking on Divinity

In ceremonial terms this is called invocation to godform; the Craft calls it channeling deity. Both systems approach this with great reverence as central to magical working, and it's a good idea to study as much as possible on the subject.

Set up your hetaera space and prepare yourself. This time set an alarm clock in the space, timed to go off two or three hours after the working begins. You may also ask a roommate or partner to tap on the door that long after you've begun.

Choose a particular piece of jewelry, a necklace or forehead circlet or bracelet, that will represent your union with the divinity.

Assume the magical personality. Seal and circle just yourself. Before your altar, repeat the prayer of dedication you've made to the Lord or Lady's service. Say, "Tonight my body shall be yours, and we will be as one." Then put on the piece of jewelry you've chosen.

Now make love with yourself, using any of the energy building and circulating techniques you're comfortable with. Imagine and feel energy rising through the central column.

Take as many climaxes as you like. With the end climax, see and sense the deity in the globe above the head, then descending into your body. Say, "I am Aphrodite" or "I am Dionysus" or the name of the deity you've chosen.

Lay still, quieting your mind as much as possible to allow the god or goddess to express themselves. The deity may grant you visions or sensations, may desire to eat or dance, may tell you what they will need from you in the future.

The sense of presence may withdraw at a certain point. If not, your alarm will go off or a knock will come at the door.

At that point, take off the piece of jewelry. Say your magical name aloud. Thank the Lord or Lady for sharing their joy with you. Finish the meal, close down the circle, and record the working.

Working with Others

Exercise: Worshiping a Deity

Partners can enact deity for one another. As with those working alone, choose a piece of jewelry that will represent you when you become the deity of your choice.

Set up a ritual meal. Assume your magical personalities. If you're acting as worshiper, seal yourself, saying, "I dedicate my body as a temple to the worship of my Lord (or Lady)." Then seal your partner, saying, "I dedicate your body as a temple for the presence of" and name the deity. Then place the piece of jewelry on your partner.

The worshipper should feed the partner who is enacting divinity. Then make love, using the energy building and circulating techniques you've grown familiar with. The worshiping partner should speak as if to the Lord or Lady. If you're enacting divinity, you may find that you will say or do things that seem unfamiliar--the Lord or Lady speaks and moves through you.

When the working is concluded, the worshiping partner should remove the jewelry that betokens the presence of divinity. Speak your magical names aloud. The worshiping partner can pay special attention to thanking the channeling partner for allowing the experience to happen.

Remember to trade positions, so both of you have the opportunity to worship a deity and become divine.

Exercise: The Divine Lovers

If you are working with a divine pair, you can choose to allow your divinities to make love with one another through your bodies. You may dedicate a session to a god or goddess, or to the union of the Lover Goddess and her younger sister/self, the Maiden, or to Lover God and his younger brother/self, the Youth. Any combination of divinity is possible. This is true of heterosexual and same-sex couples; for divinity can express itself through any physical form.

This can be a polarity working, with pairs of opposites attributed to each of the deities.

Lover Goddess: gold and red, the sun, daytime, fire, water, older.
The Maiden: silver, the moon, nighttime, air, earth, younger.

Lover God: green, the moon, nighttime, earth, water, older.
The Youth: yellow, the sun, daytime, fire, air, younger.

Set up the working as before. This time each of you may put on the jewelry that designates you as a channel for divinity.

You should again set an alarm clock to be end the trance. You might also find that your magical personalities are strong enough that you will be able to take the jewelry from one another at the completion of a working. Be certain to build in one of these mechanisms for making the transition from the channel to normal consciousness.

The Presence

Sexual energy sometimes generates a presence that doesn't seem to be the deity or pair you've chosen to work with. For a single person, this is the Other. For a couple, term hetaeras use is the Third.

Some texts call this the magical child, because the energy of a working tends to take on a life of its own. The "child", the life of the working itself, is what we use to shape the result we want: a physical thing, a change in ourselves, knowledge, contact with the divine.

The presence isn't always simply the concentrated energy of the working. What it is can be hard to pin down. We can think of it as the guardian of sex magicians; a spark of spirit; the Serpent of passion itself.

Sometimes the Other or the Third generated in magical workings attracts people to you. The solo sex magician need not stay that way for long! It's possible to shape an image of a lover, if you joke, to call one to you.

This happens for couples as well. Sometimes a person will step into that space, to become an actual third person in the relationship. Frequently one or both partners may be sexually attracted to that third. Acting on that attraction may strengthen all the relationships, or may serve to dissolve them. The third can also become the best friend, a conversationalist, a roommate, a confidant.

You may choose to acknowledge that presence with a prayer or a brief thanks during your workings. You may dedicate a working to the guidance that the presence offers.

The Higher Self

Ceremonial magicians work toward an experience described as the knowledge of the Higher Self. The Self is envisioned as a part of us, our own piece of the Spirit of All Things.

You may find, during workings, that you or your partner speak in a different voice than your normal tone, with special messages to one another, with a particular wisdom neither one of you seemed to possess before.

One way of looking at it is that being worshiped as divine has called the Self to speak through you. The hetaera's techniques form a valid path to the goal ceremonialists seek. Using the tools of our bodies we rise to the stars.

Chapter Nine: The Red Marriage

The red marriage confirms the hetaera as one who is dedicated to using sexual techniques in magical practice. It's an initiation, a marking point between one moment of our lives and another.

In hetaera time, meditate on what being a hetaera means to you, and make a journal entry.

Bathe, anoint your subtle body centers with musk or other deeply scented oils--you might have prepared an oil to use consecrated with your body fluids. As you found a white garment for the white marriage, find or make a red garment to wear just for this purpose; you may also use your hetaera robe, if it's red.

Prepare the Space

Place a red cloth on the shelf or table dedicated to your chosen deity. Decorate the image with fresh greenery and red flowers, and add a red candle and musk or heavy floral incense. Lay out a red meal.

Make sure you or you and your partner will be undisturbed for the duration of the rite. Enter your hetaera space. Put on the piece of jewelry you've chosen to represent your magical personality, repeating your magical name.

Dedication

You can choose to dedicate your pleasure to your chosen deity; partners can choose to enact sun and moon, or to channel deity during the working. Seal yourself or your partner, saying:

> *I dedicate my body as a temple to the worship of (name your deity or the energy you are representing.)*

As you touch your feet, say:

> *May I always walk the path of the hetaera.*

Touch the crown center again, saying:

May the light of divinity guide me through all my work.

The Marriage

Light the candle and incense, and read out a prayer to your chosen deities. If you've chosen to represent divinity, put on the piece of jewelry that represents the deity to you, or put the necklace or bracelet on your partner.

Red foods represent, in addition to daytime and fire energies, the passion of unleashed sexuality. Here are some ideas for red foods:

Meat: hamburger, steak. Vegetarians can choose beets, rhubarb, tomatoes.

Beans: red beans.

Dairy: berry yogurt.

Sweets: berries and berry ice cream, red candies.

Liquids: red wine, berry fruit juices.

Hold your hands over the foods and say:

May you sustain me/us in this rite and throughout my/our work.

Visualize and feel red light flowing from your hands to the foods.

Read the journal entry on your understanding of what a hetaera means. Ask your deities, and the presence which is the guardian and inspiration of hetaeras, to guide you in all workings.

Eat some of the meal, and feed some to your partner.

Now make love with yourself or your partner, bringing the energy of the working to each center in turn with each climax. Release the energy with an end-climax, sending the energy to the crown center for your success in the hetaera path.

Then visualize and sense the energies you have expended mixing together and being reabsorbed into your body and your partner's body.

Speak the words of union that come freely to you in the moment of floating freedom following the release.

Closing

You can sleep in hetaera space, and ground the working in the morning. Or when you have rested, finish the meal. Take off the jewelry representing deity and say your magical name. Then take off your magical personality piece and say your birth name. Set your garment aside, clean up the room, and return part of the meal to the earth for the deities.

Ritual Outline

Here's an outline version of the rite:
  --Self check/partner check
  --Define intention of working
  --Set up space, table and meal
  --Bathe and clothe yourself
  --Assume magical personality
  --Make sure you won't be disturbed
  --Recite dedication
  --Seal and circle
  --Magically charge food
  --Consume meal
  --Build and circulate energy
  --Release energy toward intended result
  --Reabsorb energy
  --Thank partner/divinity
  --Grounding--clean space and table
  --Record the working

Each magician follows a chosen path to the goal we seek. As hetaeras we worship the gods and strive for self-knowledge through the path of the union of love.

Appendix One : On the Word Hetaera

The word "hetaera" means companion. I have used the word here to mean practitioner of sacred sexuality, applied equally to men and women. The text defines the values I attach to sexual companionship.

In Greece the word designated a particular class of women. How that class functioned changed with geographical location and with time. Greek family structures, especially for the upper classes, differed sharply from our own, and from one another. As a general rule, women lost power steadily from archaic to classical times.

In Athens, especially in classical times, upper class women were physically confined largely to their homes. Men and slaves did the shopping. Men looked to their wives to run a household and produce children.

These were the women attracted to the worship of Dionysus. Artists too worshipped him, and Greek theater began with rituals composed in his honor.

Athenian men engaged in relationships with other men; most often this took the form of hero-worship of older men by younger ones. They turned to hetaeras for a relationship with an educated woman.

Even in classical Athens, not the most hospitable environment for strong women, hetaera exercised power over their lives. They kept their own houses and controlled their own property. They chose their lovers, some only one at a time, some several. Their lovers contributed to the running of their households--it was the hetaeras' form of income. The women passed their position from mother to daughter, hosted parties for artists and philosophers, sponsored public works projects and temple offerings. Some married, and even then insisted upon their right to make love with whomever they wished. Scholars call them prostitutes.

These people formed the educated citizenry (though women did not participate in the councils which created the laws, and were generally represented by male relatives). In the "lower" social strata, citizen wives moved more freely about the city and the countryside.

Sparta's family structure seems to have allowed women more scope to move, though modern Western women wouldn't necessarily have been comfortable there. Boys and young men lived in common barracks. Girls studied at Artemis' shrine, undertaking social training and religious initiations. They were married in their late teens, though in secret. Husbands visited their wives' family home at night, returning by day to the barracks. The couple might not set up a separate house until they were in their thirties. The men left for long periods of time on various battle campaigns, while women ran the households and some of the essential services. Here too the men bonded with one another, and took prostitutes and possibly hetaera with them on campaigns.

Across the Aegean on the island of Lesbos, girls also clustered in small social groups for training and religious activities. These groupings might last through their lifetimes, and their friendships and love relationships would survive even their marriages to men.

Hetaera are mentioned wherever the Greeks set up shop, in Italy, in Egypt, in Syria. It's hard to tell when both Greek writers and modern scholars use the word when they mean the educated women and when they mean less well-educated prostitutes, both women and boys.

Those who study sexual priesthoods, in India, Sumeria, and Babylonia, Palestine, Egypt, and the Mediterranean, call the priestesses and priests prostitutes. They do not generally differentiate between sacred and secular sexuality, and almost always view the phenomenon through the lenses of modern cultural attitudes toward prostitution.

Personally I think distinctions must be made between practitioners of sacred and secular sexuality. We must also bear in mind that the giving of money to a woman or a temple may have a different meaning for the culture, for the giver, and for the priestess or priest, and a different meaning than we would ascribe to it.

It's also easy to over-romanticize the hetaera, relieved as we can be to find among the Greeks women with some sense of self-determination. We must remember it was the men who wrote about them; their own views of what they were doing and why may again have differed substantially.

We must also differentiate between the hetaera, priestesses who held power, and those women who were engaged in sexuality who did not necessarily hold power. The temple of Aphrodite at Corinth maintained a corps of women, many of whom were slaves, who were sexually available to worshippers at the temple, including sailors drifting into the port. The men who lay with them paid the temple for the privilege, and it doesn't seem the women saw a lot of money for it. We don't know much at all about what their lives were like, or what they thought about it.

There is some indication that hetaeras were engaging in what we would recognize as sacred sexuality. They worshipped Aphrodite, who may be related to Astarte and Asherah, Semitic goddesses who had powerful sexual priesthoods. Also some of the clubs Greek men frequented, called hetaeria, were organized around the worship of non-Olympian deities.

Phyrne is a notable example. This Boetian woman rose to fame as an Athenian hetaera in the 4th century B.C. The sculptor Praxiteles based his Aphrodite on her, and the statue was placed at Aphrodite's temple at Knidus. Phryne was indicted in Athens for organizing a group of worshippers around a non-state0approved god, Isodaetes, and corrupting the morals of the youth. In her defense the orator Hyperides bared her bosom and told the assembly, here is a prophetess and seer of Aphrodite! The assembly reacted both to her beauty and with fear, and later did not allow a defendant to be present when charges were debated. This tells us something about both Phryne and Aphrodite.

Appendix Two: A Bit of History

The Near East

Cultures that flourished in the Near East five thousand years ago honored sexuality in religion and ritual.

Sumeria, the oldest culture whose writing modern scholars can read, grew up along the banks of the Tigris and Euphrates rivers in what is now Iraq. Sumerian history yields many firsts, among which can be counted "first texts on sacred sexuality".

Once a year a king of the semi-autonomous cities married, in a public ceremony and celebration, the Queen of Heaven and Earth. In private ritual at the top of the staircase temples or ziggurats, the king spent a night with a priestess of Inanna. The rite petitioned Inanna to grant the land a prosperous year and the king a prosperous life.

Sumerian culture gradually gave way to Babylonian as Semitic tribes moved into the cities. The goddess' name changed to Ishtar, but some ritual practices held over. Temples of both cultures, great sprawling bureaucratic beehives, housed several different kinds of priests and priestesses. Some of the words describing their functions haven't been translated, but some of them seem to have been sexual priestesses and possibly sexual priests, enacting some form of rite with the common folk worshipers at the temples.

Almost every researcher in the field mentions Herodotus at this point. The Greek historian says of the temples of Ishtar that every Babylonian woman had to spend one night there at some point in her life, engaging in sexuality with the first man who paid her any amount of coin to do so. Whether this account is accurate is anyone's guess.

Some of Sumeria's great cities grew out from smaller villages based on a date orchard economy. The elaborate once a year marriage ceremonies may have originated in more intimate rites held by villagers among the trees to encourage and celebrate their fertility. That seems to have been the custom in the Israel/Jordan/Palestine area. Canaanite and Israelite priestesses, and possibly priests, held rituals in tents beneath trees on the hilltops, worshiping Asherah and possibly Astarte and some of her sister goddesses. Prophets of

Yahweh preached against the custom and eventually stamped it out among the Hebrew tribes.

Not among the Canaanites, though. They became the seafaring Phoenicians, spreading colonies--and possibly ideas about sacred sexuality--throughout the Mediterranean at least. The Greek historian Herodotus mentioned one temple to Atargatis which maintained sexual priestesses.

Egypt had temples with sexual clergy as well. At least one papyrus devotes itself to an erotic encounter with a priestess of Hathor. The culture of Egypt maintained a stable, sophisticated level of civilization for several thousand years, while neighboring eastern and Mediterranean empires rose and fell. Egyptian custom had tremendous impact on the Near East and influenced Mediterranean thought. Some ceremonialists believe that modern western magick derives from that of Egypt in more or less direct succession.

The West

Contact between the cultures of east and west has been intermittent throughout the last six thousand years.

A trade network bound India's Harappan culture with Egypt, with Minoan Crete and the successor Mycenean culture on Crete and mainland Greece. While our understanding of all these cultures is fragmentary, some interesting speculation is possible. Harappans made images of a god very like later Hindu representations of Shiva; and Shiva behaves very like Dionysus, whose name at least is recorded in Mycenaean. Some commonality of understanding of sexual ritual may have been shared among the cultures.

Harappa and Mycenae fell to Indo-European invasions, and contact between the lands was severed for a time.

Greek Timeline

Minoan Crete 3000-2200 BCE
Mycenean Crete/Greece 2200-1200 B.C.E.
Dark Ages 1200-800 B.C.E.
Archaic Greece 800 400 B.C.E.
Classical Greece 400-150 B.C.E.
Roman Occupation 150 B.C.-300 CE

We know Minoan culture and religion through its art, through excavations of palaces and villages, and through surviving caves and hilltop shrines. The Minoans were non-Indo-European, and their writing remains undeciphered.

The first wave of Indo-Europeans conquered the Minoans and then assimilated some of its culture. The Mycenean culture which resulted occupied part of mainland Greece as well as Crete, and was destroyed with the second and third wave of Indo-European Greeks from the north. We can read Mycenean script, and speculate abut Minoan religion based on what we find in the Mycenean.

Greece entered a non-literate period which ended when the Phoenician script was adapted to the language. The historical curtain rises again about 800 B.C.E. The great archaic poets--Homer, Hesiod, Sappho, and others--draw upon a wealth of oral poetry transmitted through the dark ages, recalling the glories of the Mycenean culture, and their works may preserve survivals of Minoan religion.

The Greece we know best is the land during its classical period, from the wealth of plays, histories, literature and art generated from about 400 B.C.E. until the Roman conquest.

Minoan art seems to focus on images of the feminine--on priestesses and goddesses. There are also bulls and crescent--shapes which are called "horns of consecration", but there do not seem to be any really strong anthropomorphic male deific images. The Indo-Europeans brought their sky-father and a what seems to be a considerably more aggressive mode of male behavior. The grafting of Indo-European religious ideas on the Minoan religion seems to have disempowered goddesses and their priestesses.

The state-approved Greek religion seated gods and goddesses on Mount Olympus, and this is the form of the pantheon we study most deeply in school. Only some of the land's deities made it to the peak; other deities were also worshiped by citizens, farmers, hetaeras. The state-approved priesthoods, rulers and wealthier citizens occasionally felt threatened by these, and made efforts to stamp them out. This seems to have happened in Dionysus' case, though he became so popular he was finally accepted into the Olympian band. In art he sometimes appears uncomfortable there.

The West in the Common Era

Greek culture, and all of Europe, was eclipsed by the Roman empire. Roman culture wasn't terribly comfortable with Dionysian-style sexuality. Eventually, of course, Christianity swept the empire.

In the last few centuries before and the first few centuries after the common era, the Near East experienced a great confluence of cultures. A number of interesting syncretic religions evolved out of this wealth of shared information. Some sects are grouped together under the term Gnostic, with strands of Hebrew, Christian and Greek ideas woven together. Gnostic texts honor a female principle, who became less concrete than the older goddesses, more of an idea than a worshiped image. Christian detractors report Gnostic group sex rituals, though it's hard to tell whether they're reporting actual practices or simply laying sensational charges against rival religions. Gnostics may have made their way to India as well, and Gnostic ideas probably entered into that country's religious mix.

Christianity spelled doom for sexual priesthoods. In brief, goddesses were out, temples were out, sexuality was out, and all such activities either ceased or were carried out in secrecy. In the first few centuries of the common era Christianity took hold in Egypt, and the Near East was more or less held in the grip of the Eastern Orthodox church. Later, Islam swept most of that part of the world, extending into India as well. While the East maintained a higher level of culture, East and West separated as Europe entered its dark ages.

Each religion had its mystics. Islam has had the Sufis, who collected remnants of older magical understandings for some centuries. Christian mystics lived the religious life in monasteries throughout Europe.

East met West again when pilgrims began trekking back to Palestine about a thousand years ago. The order of the Knights Templar was founded to protect those pilgrims; they fought with Islamic warriors, occasionally pretending to convert to Islam in order to save their lives. It's possible that the knights had some contact with Sufic mystics.

Certainly Europe was fascinated with its glimpses of the cultured East. Grubby illiterate knights found themselves stumbling into huge Byzantine courts, surrounded by perfume and poetry, and were captivated by those splendors.

No part of the continent was more taken by the orient than Provence. The region spanned parts of France, Italy, and Spain--that

126

Brandy Williams

last country then part of the Islamic world. A whole culture evolved that was deeply influenced by Persian poetry, revolving around concepts of romantic love. The Troubadours immortalized some of their beliefs in songs. Some lyrics and melodies survive.

The people of Provence seem to have worshiped a Persian, probably Zoroastrian deity very different from the Christian god. Eventually the Church called a Crusade against the gentle singers, and the culture that supported them fell to the newest onslaught of repression.

A very interesting shadow culture developed in that part of the world in the 1300's. The Church maintained academies for the training of clergy, boys from the farm drawn to the scholar's life. Not all candidates actually made the whole course, and not all who did were placed in Church maintained positions. They took up the wandering life and developed a protective, information sharing network, making a living partly by ministering to isolated rural areas which did not have regular contact with a priest. They bore some hostility for the Church at times. It's possible that some of what we know as modern Craft ritual was developed and nurtured through that network, and it's also possible that the Church's crusade against witchcraft partly targeted that population.

In Spain, Jewish Qabalists wrote the earliest recorded treatises on the subject, again at about the same period of time. Elsewhere, Christian mystics founded the Rosicrucian and Freemasonic orders. The Rosicrucians especially worked with a male/female polarity, with some understanding of the necessity to balance male and female characteristics.

Ceremonialists trace a line of magical thought from the Knights Templar, through the Rosicrucians and Freemasons, to the members of the Golden Dawn, who framed the modern version of the system. In this line the Ordo Templi Orientis is worth noting as well; the O.T.O. became Aleister Crowley's own vehicle for magical thoughts and energy transmissions. The group's rituals revolve around an understanding of sexuality and the effects of awakening the centers of the subtle body.

What of witchcraft? If we say that history begins with written material, the Craft only really became a historical religion in this century. The religion certainly has preserved lore about connection between people and land which can be said to date from pre-Christian times, even if particulars of ritual have altered. Initiations generally pass from man to woman, woman to man; intercourse between priest and priestess is considered highly sacred. One of the

127

powers and secrets of the religion is the ability to become Lord or Lady, to "channel" deity in a group working context.

The Far East

"Tantra" describes a set of values underlying a lot of Hindu and Buddhist history. One of the things the word means is an actual text, an explanation of a religious approach.

Throughout India's history, various religions sprang up, fought, broke, merged with other sects, died off, or continued to grow to the present era. Their texts can differ from one another, and bear some similarities.

Tantric ideas probably originated with the Harappan people, non- Indo0Europeans who built a sophisticated culture in India about five thousand years ago. The Indo-European Aryans conquered the native culture, bringing a religious understanding codified in the Vedas. India's religious history traces a tension between Vedic and Tantric points of view.

Buddhism, founded in India, spread to Tibet. Though the religion died out eventually in India it flourished in the mountain country, overlaid on Bon and other older religions.

Indian texts in general were and written in Sanskrit; Tibetan monasteries preserved copies of these that were later lost in India. These were translated into Tibetan. Schools schismed from one another, teachers wrote original Tibetan works, and the Tantric tradition in that country took on a unique character.

The British occupation of India brought English speakers into close contact with the Hindu Tantras, and the texts began to be translated into that language. Since the Chinese occupation of Tibet, Buddhists texts have also been steadily translated into English. The amount of material available in that language, though, is only a fraction of what has actually been written.

Only a handful of scholars in the world read both Sanskrit and Tibetan. Some Hindu texts are also written in a Dravidian language, Tamil. Comparisons of the systems, and even clear understandings of them, come slowly because of the language and culture barrier.

Those who venture to read the English translations can discover whole new vistas of obscure language. For example, some translators of Tibetan texts sprinkle their work liberally with more commonly understood Sanskrit terms, even though they're not present in the original. Almost every Sanskrit translator gives up on a few hundred words and simply uses them in English sentences, hoping the reader will pick them up from repetition and context.

Even where English words are used, they're not necessarily illuminating; "the first of the four bliss-voids" leaves me wondering how the four bliss-voids differ from one another.

Ceremonial magicians acquired access to the Sanskrit Tantras at the end of the last century. Arthur Avalon wrote several largish works on the subject, and Aleister Crowley was deeply affected by the concepts. The O.T.O. also worked with some of the yogic and sexual techniques.

All this access to information spawned a whole new genre of popular English literature: occult sex manuals. The number of books on the market has increased noticeably with the blossoming of the human potentials movement and the new age network.

All this forms the historical and cultural heritage for the modern practitioner of sacred sexuality. As more people study the history, read the texts, experiment with lines of thought and write about them, we continue to build a western-based set of texts generating a modern, native English body of knowledge.

Appendix Three: Sex Magick Ethics

The hetaera's ethics can be summed up in a single phrase: sex magick requires consent. In various situations this can mean informing or educating your partner, making sure your partner can give consent, and thinking through the goal you want the sex magick to accomplish. It means being honest with yourself and those whose energy you share, and more, caring about what happens to all the people you touch.

Ethic: You have the right to say yes to sex

You own your sexuality. No person, no deity, no law, no religion, or philosophy has the right to tell you how you should express your sexual self. Who you choose as your partner, where you choose to make love, and how you explore your sensual and energic self are all totally your decisions to make.

The hetaera would add that this is so within the bounds of sex magick ethics. So long as all parties you contact sexually have consented to the sex, wherever your sexuality leads you is strictly your own path.

Ethic: You have the right to say no to sex

You own your body. You own your touch. You have the right to defend yourself from others who wish to touch you without your permission. No one has the right to demand sexuality from you for any reason. This is true of people in positions of authority, family members, teachers, clergy; legal spouses; boyfriends and girlfriends; spirit entities and deities. If you don't want to, don't.

Enforcing that "no" may require drawing a line that you are not used to drawing. Remember that you are defending your right to live your life in safety, and defending your right to direct your own energy to your own spiritual benefit.

Ethic: Every participant in a sex magick working must agree to the sex magick and the intended purpose of the energy

This ethic covers the topic of consent for the energy work as well as consent for the sex. It can seem awkward to bring up the subject with a new partner, but it is as important a conversation to have with your partners as the conversation about safe sex. An inexperienced partner may choose to permit you to direct the energy of the working. You can also incorporate simple energy techniques as part of your intimate play, a way to get to know each other.

This doesn't mean that every partner will benefit equally from the working. Partners may choose to donate their energy. When one partner has a significant physical issue, bringing that person back to health may be the focus of the sex magick for quite some time. In healthy relationships though this should even out over time, so that both partners receive some of the benefits of the energy work.

Specifically, this means that hetaeras do not expect one partner, whether female (most often) or male (it happens) to act only as the support for the other partner's magical development. Both partners of whatever sex and whatever their relative skill levels are fundamentally equals in the relationship.

Ethic: True power exchange can only happen between equals

Our daily lives contain many situations in which we hold power over others or in which others hold power over us. Examples of uneven power relationships include: bosses and employees, teachers and students, doctors and patients. When sex occurs between two people in any of these relationships the question of consent arises: because one of the parties holds a real power over the other, there is an element of coercion, whether it is overtly stated or even intended.

The wisest course of action is to wait until the relationship changes before engaging in sex. In humans lust and love strikes without caring whether the object of our affections is suitable. In that case the best resolution to the situation is to end the power relationship. If that is not immediately possible, both parties should strive to remain as clear as possible and to compensate for the power imbalance with honesty, caring, and the sharing of power. That said, however scrupulous you are, the question whether full consent can occur between unequal partners always remains in the air.

Of course if a teacher, doctor, or employer initiates unwelcome sexual contact, this is a form of coercion, and you have the responsibility to yourself to resist in every way possible.

Ethic: Sex magick should only happen between consenting adults

Sex with children is one of the great scourges of our time--there are few crimes as heinous. It imprints the experience on the child at the deepest level; abuse survivors can recover to lead normal, healthy sexual lives, but the abuse is always there as a factor to be managed. Since children do not fully understand sex, and since, the power exchange between children and adults is never equal, children cannot consent, and any sexual encounter involves a form of coercion.

This is also true for animals. Cross-species communication is difficult at its best. Since you cannot tell whether the animal understands what you want or what is happening, consent is impossible to determine. You also stand in an unequal power relationship with pets and livestock which you exploit when we initiate sex.

Feedback

In my travels around the country teaching about sex magick, the topic that has caused the most discussion is ethics. At one lecture when I said "you have the right to say no," a woman in the audience pulled me aside at the break and said, "I am not going back to my house." The lecture organizers were able to find a shelter to take her in for the night.

Usually responses are not quite so dramatic, but can be spirited. Gay men sometimes object when I say "All partners should know about the sex magick and agree to the working," pointing out that group sex encounters, such as those in bath houses, occur in a very different context than one to one partnerships. Some feel that partners in group sex environments have already given their permission for energy work to occur without the need for discussion, and point out that sexual encounters might occur between partners in those situations who never speak.

Brandy Williams

Magical people in long-term relationships with non-magical people sometimes wonder how to bring up the topic. They ask me if they can just circle and seal their partners without explaining what they are doing. Again, this is a conversation that can help partners learn about each other. Also, unless you have that conversation, your partner is always at a disadvantage, never getting to choose where the energy is going. Even if you scrupulously share out the energy, making sure your partner benefits, you have still missed an opportunity to share, and have entered into an unequal power relationship.

Some sex magick systems deliberately teach magicians how to take energy from others. Some texts describe methods for approaching children and young people and siphoning off their energy, not through direct physical contact, but with energy movement techniques. Other texts instruct male magicians to find unintelligent but physically healthy women to act as uninformed partners, and to treat them as magical tools rather than as people.

It is my hope that the system of sex magick developed here, with its emphasis on the unity of body, mind, heart, and spirit, will help contribute to the development of sex magick ethics, so that sex magick becomes, not a way to denigrate, rob, or harm others, but instead serves as a source of pleasure, health, and joy for everyone we touch.

Appendix Four : Tantric Masturbation

Laughing Otter (James Moore) first published this essay in the small press journal Wiggansnatch *in 1984. It was picked up by TOPY (Temple of Psychic Youth) and appeared in newsgroups in the early 1990s.*

This was my first attempt to describe the system of I had developed for use on my own and later with my partner. It is still my most personal writing on sex magick. After I submitted a first draft to James he called me and said, "This is too impersonal. Tell me what you do. Tell me how you feel." This is the result.

James was my first editor. He encouraged me to take myself seriously as a writer, for which I will always be grateful. He died of AIDs related complications in the 1980s, a loss to the magical and literary communities. I still miss him.

Tantric Masturbation

I prefer an outside location against the base of a friendly tree, or on a deserted beach. Where I now live, I have access to a large shower with a carpet and a big soft upholstered lounge chair that works well.

My greatest success happens during my moontime (when I am menstruating.) At that time I feel a substantial quantitative increase in the internal heat generated by this technique.

Sealing

To seal means to close the chakras (the energy centers of the aura) and the body orifices, with a touch and a visualization. I lightly touch my fingertips to the top of my head, forehead, eyes, nose, ears, mouth, throat, between my breasts, solar plexus, genitals, anus and feet. With each touch I visualize a circle closing, like the petals of a flower closing for the night. I finish the seal by drawing a circle around myself. I pass my hands over my heart center, over my head, along my body, under my feet, and back to my heart center. At the same time I visualize a blue light trailing from my fingertips, making a blue oval to enclose me.

When I seal before masturbating or making love, I feel an increase of heat in my heart and genitals; and I don't feel tired or drained or lonely or scared when I'm done - I feel warm and cherished, by myself or by my partner. I also find that if I do not seal or protect myself during my moontime, I experience a much more severe exhaustion after using this technique, a 'loss of energy' similar to that which my partner describes when he ejaculates frequently.

Tantric writers often say that male bodies must conserve their energy, but that female bodies may give endlessly; from my experience I do not find that statement to be true. Female bodies also lose fluids.

Breathing Rhythmically

I use a 6-3-6-3 pattern. I inhale for six heartbeats, hold the air in my lungs for three heartbeats, exhale for six, and rest without breathing for three. An easier and more common pattern is to inhale for four beats and exhale four beats. Whenever I do any kind of magick, I use this breath pattern, so for me it's linked to feeling sacred and powerful. It also makes me breathe more deeply, which relaxes me. Breathing meditation in general helps me clear my mind. Later, there will be a tim e to generate images. For now, I want to clear out extraneous material. I'm not going to think about the article I'm writing or what I'm making for dinner. I'm going to make love to myself, and only that. The breathing helps me to concentrate.

Autoerotic Stimulation

The first step in actually making self-love is to stimulate myself and watch while I'm doing it. I'm not talking about just stimulation of the clitoris (or penis) by hand - I rub my body against the surface I'm on - earth or sand or soft cloth. I stroke the whole of my body, and suck whatever I can comfortably reach with my mouth. The quality of this touch is light, gentle and cherishing...which doesn't mean that it isn't passionate, only that it is not perfunctory or violent.

Heightened Pleasure

Just before I climax, I stop. I visualize a column of gold or white energy rising from my genitals to my heart center hot. When I stop the physical stimulation just short of contraction, I get some of the same effects as in full-orgasm. I feel sensation in my clitoris, a sense of my body trembling slightly, a brief cessation of thought, and perhaps one or two very small vaginal contractions. My partner experiences similar effects, including penile contractions. However, I don't allow myself a full set of contractions, and he doesn't allow himself ejaculation. We call this "climax without ejaculation" and "climax without contractions." Obviously, our language isn't set up to discuss this.

This (hopefully specific) description does not convey the pleasure of the experience. This is a smaller-scaled orgasm, not as intense or as uncontrollable as a full orgasm, but still fun. When I start a session, I require some stimulation and time to climax (without contraction) the first three times. Thereafter, I experience a sort of perpetual state of almost-climax (with contraction). I become very physically quiet, limiting stimulation to clitoris only, and hit a series of peaks of intense pleasure.

Parenthetically, my partner reports a very recent experience. He's getting a climax with partial ejaculation. He reports the sensations and penile contractions are slightly less intense than all-out orgasm. The ejaculate is a different color: clear, not white. There is no loss of erection or arousal. We don't know what's going on here biologically. It is, at this point, an involuntary experience. The advantage of being able to make love while retaining a more or less indefinite state of arousal is obvious. Tantric masturbation is a good place to learn, where no one will be upset if you go over the edge, and where the learning can progress more quickly because you're in complete control.

Visualization:

The second stage of making love to myself is to generate imagery. I close my eyes and lift my head so that my spine is more or less straight. In my mind's eye, I see a column of gold or white light rising from my genitals, along my spine, through the chakras, and out through the top of my head to a globe two or three hand-widths above. At the same time I feel an increase of internal heat where the column passes, until my central body, from genitals to head, is a flame.

Some people refer to this as "rousing Kundalini." They visualize the flame as a serpent raising its body. This is supposed to bring enlightenment. It is also supposed to make the entire body shake uncontrollably, and to be dangerous to do without the guidance of a master. I experienced that kind of reaction once. It did frighten me. I stopped, and it immediately went away. I have a friend who experienced this kind of vibration in a chakra meditation and thought, 'Wonderful! I'm doing something right.' So I think that what a guide might do is explain that the reaction is normal and safe.

Indian Tantric mythology talks about a dancer, Shiva, and his snake, Shakti. They create the Universe. I know another myth: Eurynome, the Goddess, who danced in The Void and formed Ophion, the Snake, from the wind. They created the Universe also.

I use both images. The idea is to raise the Kundalini in my spine (the snake) up to my crown chakra (the dancer) and to unite them. The snake coils around the dancer's legs, body, genitals, and chest, licking the dancer's face. I imagine how a snake would feel coiled around my own body of light, slippery, and moist with my sweat, undulating rhythmically. Alternatively, I see a being of light whose outlines dissolve in radiance, neither male nor female, remote from me, infinitely compassionate, with me and yet apart, stretching hands out to almost touch me, imparting great love and wisdom.

Annotated Bibliography

In the mid-1800s and early 1900s, several writers, including Sir John Woodruffe and Aleister Crowley, brought eastern philosophy and ritual to the west. These writers were the first wave in the modern western sex magick tradition. They combined Eastern techniques, mostly termed Tantric, including chakras, energy work, and embodying deity, with Western alchemy, occult Qabbalah derived from Jewish and Christian philosophical traditions, demonic grimoires, and practical methodologies such as sigil magick.

A second wave of writers in the 1970s and 1980s updated the western sex magick tradition with additional information and techniques deriving from a more detailed reading of the eastern traditions. Nearly all second wave books were written by men working in the Golden Dawn, Ordo Templi Orientis, or other formal Western Ceremonial Magick orders. These books often treat women with condescension and aim their primary message at white male heterosexual readers with women partners. In this time period the term "Tantra" became more or less synonymous with "sex magick."

In the late 1990s and early 2000s new writers began to explore new avenues of sex magick. While new wave writers can still be male-centered and heterosexist, these works generally make some attempt to address diversity issues. More women writers emerged in this time period. The new wave approaches sex magick in a more holistic and balanced fashion than its predecessors, combining emotion, and emerging sciences, and sex positive techniques with magical training and goals.

First Wave Work

Avalon, Arthur (Sir John Woodroffe). *Shakti and Shakta*. New York: Dover Publications, Inc., 1978. First published in London, 1918.
---. The Serpent Power. New York: Dover Publications, 1974. First published in London, 1919.

These books were among the first to bring eastern ideas to a western audience. Then as now more useful for education than as practical manuals.

Brandy Williams

Pascal Beverly Randolph

Deveney, John Patrick. *Pascal Beverly Randolph: A Nineteenth-Century Black American Spiritualist, Rosicrucian, and Sex Magician*. New York: Suny Press, 1996.

A thorough biography of an important contributor to the western sex magick tradition.

Godwin, Joscelyn, Christian Chanel and John P. Deveney. *The Hermetic Brotherhood of Luxor, Initiatic and Historical Documents of an Order of Practical Occultism*. York Beach: Samuel Weiser, Inc., 1995.

An invaluable collection of historical documents describing the workings of a nineteenth century order. Their techniques owed a great deal to the work of Pascal Beverly Randolph.

Randolph, Pascal Beverly. *Sexual Magic*. Robert North, translator and editor. New York: Magical Childe Publishing, Inc. 1988.

Describes Randolph's sex magick system that was so influential in the nineteenth and early twentieth century.

Aleister Crowley

Crowley himself did not write a how-to manual of sex magick. However, much of his life's work centers on the subject. Many of his works discuss the chakras and energy work. The order which he shaped, the Ordo Templi Orientis, works with the chakras through its initiatory system.

Urban, Hugh. "Unleashing The Beast, Aleister Crowley, Tantra and Sex Magick in Late Victorian England." Ohio State University, 2003.
http://www.esoteric.msu.edu/VolumeV/Unleashing_the_Beast.htm

Urban analyzes Crowley's understanding of eastern religious ritual as well as his crucial impact on the development of Western sex magick.

The works cited below can be found in a number of sources in print and online.

Liber XV, The Gnostic Mass

O.T.O. bodies (chapters) perform this ritual privately and publicly. It revolves around the interaction of the priest and priestess in a rite filled with sexual symbolism.

Liber XXXVI, The Star Sapphire

This sex magick ritual is written entirely in code. For an explanation of the code, see:
"Liber XXXVI The Star Sapphire, Ritual by Aleister Crowley Analysis by Frater Osiris 2003."
http://www.hermetic.com/osiris/analysisstarsapphire.htm

Second Wave Work

Crowley, Aleister, Lon Milo DuQuette and Christopher S. Hyatt, Ph.D. Enochian World of Aleister Crowley, Enochian Sex Magick. Tempe: New Falcon Publications, 1991.

A very good introduction to Enochian magick as well as the first (and possibly the only) book on Enochian sex magick.

Culling, Louis. *A Manual of Sex Magick*. St. Paul: Llewellyn Publications, 1971

Important second wave work which contains practical instructions, information about Eastern Tantric practice, and a very handy translation of alchemical terms into sex magick terms. A difficult book for women as the female practitioner is directed to subordinate her desires and energies to the male magician's control.

Denning, Melitta Denning and Osborne Phillips. *The Magick of Sex*. St. Paul: Llewellyn Publications, 1982.

A charming second wave book addressing couples in love. One of the first books to clearly discuss male multiple orgasms.

Brandy Williams

Hyatt, Christopher S., PhD. *Secrets of Western Tantra, The Sexuality of the Middle Path*. Tempe: New Falcoln Publications, 1989.

Although this bills itself as a Tantric text, it is primarily focused on Ceremonial techniques applied to a sex magick context.

Hyatt, Christopher S. and Lon Milo DuQuette. *Sex Magick, Tantra and Tarot, The Way of the Secret Lover*. Tempe: New Falcon Publications, 1991.

While based on first wave Tantric information and influenced by Aleister Crowley, this work experiments with the use of Tarot. Sex magick rituals in this work treat male and female partners as equal participants in the rites.

Mumford, Dr. John. *Sexual Occultism, The Sorcery of Love in Practice and Theory*. St. Paul: Llewellyn Publications 1975.

Another second wave book describing Tantric sexual techniques. This book also compares Shakti Tantra with Wicca and speaks about women in more respectful terms.

New Wave Work

Ashcroft-Nowicki, Dolores. *The Tree of Ecstasy, An Advanced Manual of Sexual Magic*. York Beach: Samuel Weiser, 1999.

A welcome addition to women's voices in sex magick. Ashcroft-Nowicki's strength is in visualization and in applying sex magick workings to the Tree of Life.

Ellwood, Taylor and Lupa. *Kink Magic, Sex Magick Beyond Vanilla*. Stafford: Megalithica Books, 2007.

This is the first full-length work to combine BDSM (bondage, dominance, sado-masochism) techniques with sex magick. Written by a couple, this book focuses on energetic techniques which treat relationships as important as magical accomplishments.

Kraig, Donald Michael. *Modern Sex Magick, Secrets of Erotic Spirituality*. St. Paul: Llewellyn, 2001.

The cover also specifies "with contributions by Linda Falorio, Nema, Tara, Lola Babalon," making this one of the first books to enlist women to speak as authorities on women's experience. Kraig was also one of the first writers to discuss BDSM techniques and energy direction in group sex workings.

Tyson, Donald. *Sexual Alchemy, Magical Intercourse with Spirits*. St. Paul: Llewellyn, 2000.

Tyson's work focuses on sex magick conducted with non-physical lovers, including gods and goddesses, angels and other spirits, and created entities.

U.D., Frater. Secrets of Western Sex Magick. St. Paul: Llewellyn, 2001.

Like Tyson, Frater U.D. discusses sex with deities. In a welcome change from heterosexist work, he also discusses autoerotic and homoerotic techniques.

Urban, Hugh B. *Tantra: Sex, Secrecy, Politics, and Power in the Study of Religion*. Berkley: University of California Press, 2003.

The first comprehensive history of the idea of Tantra as it entered into the West. Urban seeks to disentangle the eastern philosophical and religious system from western misunderstandings and glosses. In this work Urban discusses, among other things, Sir John Woodruffe's impact on western thought.

---. Magia Sexualis: *Sex, Magick, and Liberation in Modern Western Esotericism*. University of California Press, 2006.

The first academic history of the development of western sex magick. Among other topics Urban discusses the contributions of Pascal Beverly Randolph, Aleister Crowley, and Gerald Gardner.

Index

Did You Like What You Read?

Kink Magic: Sex Magic Beyond Vanilla by Taylor Ellwood and Lupa
978-1-905713-11-0/MB0112
$21.99/£12.99 paperback
Sex magic is a hot topic—but what about those of us who like flavors besides vanilla? A practical, innovative guide to combining BDSM, fetishes, and magical practice.

Ecstasia: A Practical Introduction to Transcendental Music and Dance by Julia R. Zay
ISBN 978-1-905713-10-3/MB0119
$21.99/£12.99 paperback
A guide to ecstastic dance based on Mediterranean traditions. For novices, ritual performers, and those who simply enjoy music and dance.

Sekhem Heka: A Natural Healing and Self-Development System by Storm Constantine
ISBN 978-1905713-13-4 / MB0114
$21.99/£12.99 paperback
Egyptian healing techniques and Reiki are elements of this dynamic system for healing on all levels of the self, created by the author.

Ogam: Weaving Word Wisdom by Erynn Rowan Laurie
ISBN 978-1-905713-02-8 / MB0110
$21.99/£12.99 paperback
Ogam isn't just about the trees! Erynn Rowan Laurie, Celtic reconstructionist elder, shares her years of experience with this well-researched, practical text.

Find these and the rest of our current lineup at
http://www.immanion-press.com